COACH OF THE BUILDING

Written by
Julian Costa

Library of Congress Cataloging-in-Publication Data:

Names:	Costa, Julian Thomas, 1989–, author
Title:	Coach of the Building
ISBN-13:	978-1-957863-34-4
BISAC:	BIO019000 BIOGRAPHY & AUTOBIOGRAPHY / Educators

Copyeditor/Proofreader:	Angel Ackerman
Layout Design:	Julian Costa
Printer and Binder:	Ingram Sparks

Photography credits are listed in the reference section.
All photos are used for editorial purposes only.
Cover Photo: Julian Costa, July 2022.

Parisian phoenix
PUBLISHING

CONNECT with the publisher:
Substack: parisianphoenixpublishing.substack.com

Web:	www.ParisianPhoenix.com
Facebook:	@parisianphoenixpublishing
Instagram:	@parisianphoenix
LinkedIn:	@parisianphoenixpublishing
Patreon:	@parisianphoenix
TikTok:	@parisianphoenix

Published by Parisian Phoenix Publishing, Easton, Pennsylvania USA
Printed in the United States of America.

TABLE OF CONTENTS

DEDICATION

This book is dedicated to

Richard O. Carty

INTRODUCTION

June, 2004. On a sunny afternoon, spirited applause filled Pennsylvania's Mountain Laurel Center as the graduates of East Stroudsburg High School North filed into the amphitheater. As the concert band performed "Pomp and Circumstance," parents' eyes filled with tears, faculty members smiled proudly, and the senior class reflected on their academic journey.

Following the singing of the National Anthem, sporting a blue tie, the principal of the school approached the lectern to offer a warm welcome. A respectful silence hushed the crowd. The principal looked out at the graduates, as he had done at previous graduations, but this group was different. They were the first to complete grades nine through twelve at the East Stroudsburg High School North. They were the pioneers of a new school and creators of a new culture, helping make decisions that would shape the future of the school and its programs. Over those four special years, the principal listened closely to their ideas, encouraged them to contribute, and attempted to get to know them personally. The principal's name was Richard Carty.

It is not uncommon for a high school principal to form a special connection with a graduating class after spending four years watching them grow, mature, and achieve. What is rare to experience is being tasked with the opening of a new high school. Carty had the unique opportunity to experience this, and the 2004 graduates earning their diplomas — thirty years after Carty earned his — were integral to the success of this school's opening.

The Pocono Mountains of northeastern Pennsylvania saw rapid change and influx during the latter years of the twentieth century. What was previously considered a vacation destination had quickly taken on a suburban culture, largely due to families moving to Pennsylvania from New York City. This placed a burden on the local school districts, which, by the mid-1990s, were very crowded. Unfortunately, not everybody viewed this as a positive change. In spite of this, Carty embraced the opportunity to develop a new school community and celebrated the diverse contributions of everyone involved. After nearly two decades of working in an established high school situated in the center of East Stroudsburg, Carty transitioned to a rural environment where he was tasked with opening a new high school and eliminating the negative perceptions being voiced throughout the community.

As a school principal, Carty strove to be approachable, collaborative, and supportive to his staff and the student body. He had no interest in upward mobility but instead he wanted to be a steadfast presence, giving students as many opportunities to succeed as possible. Beginning his career as a child counselor, Carty worked his way to principal. Today, more than a decade after his retirement, Carty is remembered by many for his leadership style, the respect he showed, and his success as a coach and as an administrator.

This book is more than a biography. In addition to sharing Carty's story, it shares the growth and modernization of a school district through times of diversification, technological advancement, and societal change. It is also intended to impart some lessons on how to bring out the best in others, a quality that is vital for any leader to possess. More specifically, this book provides a glimpse into Carty's thirty-one years in the East Stroudsburg Area School District, and hopefully, a sense of the place and time where Carty served. Not all of the topics mentioned in this book are direct contributions or accomplishments of Carty, however, they provide a necessary context to understand how and why certain things happened the way that they did. The book emphasizes Carty's years at East Stroudsburg High School North, where he served as the school's first principal. You will notice a lot of quotes have been included throughout this book, as a goal of mine was to include as many different voices and perspectives as possible.

The success of any project like this is impossible without the input and support of many individuals. First and foremost, I want to thank Richard Carty for his unwavering assistance over the past four years of research and writing, answering countless text messages and offering insight however he could. Mrs. Rose Skidmore, retired records secretary for the East Stroudsburg Area School District, was extremely helpful in providing access to meeting minutes and year-books and was always willing to share a laugh. Mrs. Susan Wilson, who served as East Stroudsburg North's first librarian, offered encouragement and feedback throughout the writing process. Mr. Mark Brown, retired Director of Athletics for the East Stroudsburg Area School District, provided historical clarification. I would also like to express my appreciation to the faculty and staff members of the East Stroudsburg Area School District — both presently serving and retired — who have contributed to this book. Finally, to my fellow alumni who have shared memories or loaned me artifacts from your school days, I greatly appreciate your help.

It is important to specify that this book is not a commissioned project, nor is it endorsed by any academic institution. This has been written as a way of giving back to my alma mater by sharing the story of its first principal. I am also aware that my historical knowledge of certain time periods may be vague, and any mistakes or erroneous information is my fault and mine only.

A few notes on usage: the name of East Stroudsburg Area Senior High School, sometimes abbreviated to "East Stroudsburg," was changed to East Stroudsburg Area Senior High School South in 2000. Bushkill Elementary School is sometimes referred to as "Bushkill" for short, and the East Stroudsburg Area Senior High School North is referred to as "East Stroudsburg High School North," "East Stroudsburg North," "the North High School," or "ENS," which was a nickname for the school used at the time.

In some of the interviews, Carty is identified by his nickname, "Rico." The source of each image, if known, is provided. All images are included for editorial use only.

For those readers who graduated from East Stroudsburg High School North, I hope that this book teaches you about the school you attended and the many individuals, including Richard Carty, who contributed to its growth over the past twenty-five years. For those of you who aspire to be a coach, a teacher, a school principal, or simply to be a leader, an innovator, and a mentor to others, hopefully this book will be a source of inspiration for you.

Julian Costa
June, 2025

STEPPING UP TO THE PLATE

Play ball! shouted the coach.

Nine youngsters eagerly ran onto the baseball field. The warm summer sun poured on the green grass, backdropped by brick buildings and busy streets. Parents and siblings cheered from the bleachers while the boys enjoyed one of America's greatest past times. CRACK, went the bat, and the coach yelled to his outfielders, "catch it!" The fly ball landed in a young player's glove. His name was Richard Carty.

From a young age, Carty had a passion for sports. His father, Richard "Dick" Carty, Sr., coached little league baseball, football, and was later an umpire for the Pennsylvania Interscholastic Athletic Association. Additionally, he was an educator.

"My father was a vocational education teacher," said Carty. "He worked in a factory and went back to school later in life. He got his vocational ed degree from Temple University and ended up teaching warehousing." Another one of Carty's most beloved role models was his mother, Lois Ann Carty, who worked hard as a shoe store manager while raising her children to be caring, compassionate members of society.

The town of Easton, Pennsylvania, located at the confluence of the Delaware and Lehigh Rivers, was like any other suburban town of the 1960s. Carty grew up on the south side of town with his five siblings. It was several miles from here where he attended school. Enrollment was booming in the Easton School District. "You had a lot of different areas that fed into the school, and sometimes you got treated differently based on what part of town you came from," Carty remembers. The faculty were caring but strict, enforcing good study habits. Unfortunately, not all students embraced these lessons right away.

One example of this was Carty's eighth-grade health education course at the junior high school. Week after week, the students in the course earned failing grades on quizzes, which continuously disappointed the teacher. What can be done to motivate a group of teenagers to study? Eventually, the teacher decided to implement "The Memory Board," which was a wooden paddle, intended to motivate the students to retain the curriculum a bit better. I will leave it to you to imagine how he used it. "The scores went up after that," Carty recalls. "I got swatted, but it was for an 80 out of 100%." Fortunately, nobody ended up failing health class that year.

Carty's teachers instilled a caring toughness in him, earning his respect but not without frustration along the way. One of these educators was Bill Houston. "He was originally from Easton, an all-American athlete and a great guy," said Carty. Houston, who began his teaching career as a junior high science and physical education teacher, later became an intermediate school principal, becoming Easton Area School District's first African-American principal.

Another teacher that Carty met during his junior high school years was Alfredean Jones. "Mr. Jones was sometimes hard to understand, he had a heavy southern accent—he was originally from North Carolina," Carty recalls. Both Houston and Jones would become role models to Carty even more than he ever could have imagined.

I had respect for them. They eventually became administrators in the school district. I ended up doing everything they did. They had that much influence on me. With them, everything was about right and wrong, regardless of what color someone's skin was. Prejudice is a learned behavior; I didn't learn it.

The grounds of Easton High School, 1971.

Years later, Carty ran into Houston at the Lehigh Valley Mall, where he was talking to one of Carty's classmates. "Someone said to [Houston], 'man, you know everybody!' He responded, 'these are my boys! I raised these boys!' Enough said."

In the fall of 1970, Carty enrolled at Easton High School. The large complex, located near the Lehigh Valley Thruway, was unfortunately prone to an unspoken separation of the social classes among the student body. "I was from south Easton, which was one of the worst sections," said Carty. "I was talking to a girl at a party, about typical high school stuff. 'What do you do, where do you live,' this and that. And I thought we were getting along pretty well." Then, the girl asked Carty where he was from, to which he replied, "south side." Without saying another word, the girl walked away. "I thought that wasn't right," remembers Carty. "She thought she was a better person because she lives in a different side of town? That stuck with me, and I never wanted to be like that."

Regardless, Carty made friends and enjoyed his high school years. Overseeing this miniature town was Mr. Phil Spaziani, who Carty remembers as "a legend at that time. He was a very good principal. He had a really good personality, very good with students."

Like many high school students, Carty was given some flexibility in choosing his coursework. For one of his elective credits, he had the choice between a course in typing or a course in public speaking. "I had taken typing in junior high school, and the teacher was tough. She'd come up behind you and say, 'feet flat on the floor! Fingers on the home row! Back straight in the chair! I hated that class."

Top: *Easton High School, 1972*
Above: *Mr. Phil Spaziani, Principal*

Though keyboarding did not become Carty's favorite class, he enjoyed the others, particularly social studies, because it provided a helpful foundation for studying not only the past, but the present.

The 1970s are often characterized as having social unrest due to racism, politics, and international conflicts. For residents of Easton, Pennsylvania, a day that will forever stand out is April 30, 1971, when, as described by reporters, "all hell broke loose." On that Friday afternoon, a fight broke out in the High School between two students, one of whom was white, and the other happened to be Black. The one teacher on the scene, who happened to be white, attempted to break up the fight. According to a 2020 article looking back on that day, "the cousin of the Black student jumped on the white teacher to try and free the Black student," and was then followed by the teacher, who "jack[ed] the Black student up against the wall."

This was only the beginning of what became a very dangerous situation. Even the principal, Spaziani, described it as "one of the most frightening scenes he's ever witnessed." Even after the situation was under control, feelings of fear and tension lingered on campus. "I was a freshman," recalls Carty, "and on our way to baseball practice we were screened by the National Guard just to get on campus."

Throughout his education, Carty continued to play sports, developing close friendships with his teammates. As his freshman year came to close, football tryouts for Easton's Red Rovers arrived. The coach, Wayne Grube, recognized Carty's talent and picked him for the 1971 junior varsity team. The team spent the summer on the field, learning plays and forming a close bond.

"I came out of a big high school where it was not easy to even be on a team in a school that size," said Carty. "Easton High School was deep in tradition, sports, and winning. Learn how to win, [and] nobody was more competitive than me."

After football season was over, Carty hung up his helmet and replaced it with a bat, as his first season on the Red Rovers' baseball team was quickly approaching. Having an interest in baseball since childhood, Carty tried out and was picked for the team. Carty quickly developed a positive rapport with his coach, James Wolbach, who is remembered as a strong, energetic coach.

From left to right: James Grube, Football Coach and James Wolbach, Baseball Coach

Above: Easton High 1973
Baseball Team
Right: Carty (#10) in the
1973 Football Team Photo
(detail)

During his high school years, Carty was invited to volunteer as a little league baseball coach. Drawing from the strong examples provided by his coaches, Carty set out to help the young players develop good sportsmanship, proper technique, and most importantly, have fun along the way.

Carty's own high school athletic career ended with ample acclaim. He earned five varsity letters, three in baseball and two in football.

As the 1973–74 school year grew shorter, the questions that many seniors ponder popped into Carty's mind, and that is, what is the next chapter going to be? He feared the idea of this decision being made for him by the armed forces. "I had a draft card, but they ended the draft just about the time I graduated high school."

Carty knew that he did not want to go to war, especially considering that several kids from his neighborhood were in Vietnam. With the encouragement of his family, and the positive mentorship he received from so many teachers and coaches, Carty declared that he wanted to go to college. Just before graduating high school, he received the news of his acceptance to Mansfield State College.

On June 9, 1974, the high school band began to play Sir Edgar Elgar's famous "Pomp and Circumstance" march as the 600-plus graduates of the class of 1974 walked onto the football field. This warm day at Cottingham Stadium was full of emotion: pride, excitement, sadness, and uncertainty. As the graduates walked across the stage, they were also walking into a world that was littered with problems. For some, the objective was to help solve some of these problems by seeking education or vocational training. Others, who took a more pragmatic approach, sought to find a job, and settle down.

Despite the unsettling tenor of the times, Carty and his fellow graduates took comfort in knowing that they did, in fact, have options and were equipped to pursue them.

Mansfield State College, which is part of today's Commonwealth University of PA.

The summer months of 1974 passed quickly by and colleges across the country prepared to welcome their incoming freshmen classes. A young college student named William George Butler penned the lyrics that would eventually become the alma mater for his institution, beginning with "Old Mansfield high upon the Eastern hill, Dear Mansfield hail to thee!" It was on this hill that Mansfield State College sat, near the northern border of Pennsylvania and New York, nearly two hundred miles from Easton. It was in the summer of 1974 Carty made the three-hour drive to Mansfield, where he enrolled for his freshman year of college. He chose Mansfield because he liked the idea of "going away to college" instead of staying close to home. Inspired by the many dedicated teachers and coaches he had encountered through his education, Carty decided to major in secondary education.

Classes began on August 28, 1974. Mansfield State College offered numerous options for teacher certification, particularly for those interested in teaching at the high school level. According to their catalog,

> The Secondary Education Department is the professional school established to conduct and coordinate, within the College, programs for the preparation of secondary school teachers. Completion of the program will graduate students with a provisional certificate to teach in the Commonwealth of Pennsylvania.

After considering the possibility of pursuing certification in speech, English, the sciences, and other areas, Carty elected to specialize in social studies. "I liked history. I still do," said Carty. "I wasn't really good at math, so that was never going to be my thing. The reason is probably because I had really good history teachers in high school. I respected them."

The curriculum required him to complete courses in American history, European history, non-Western histories, and electives from other disciplines within the social sciences such as economics or political science, which Carty greatly enjoyed. Of particular interest to Carty was the required course in educational psychology. Students in Carty's program had to complete a core sequence of courses in educational theory, audio-visual communication, and media production. Carty also got his first taste of computing when he enrolled in an Introduction to Fortran course.

Like all undergraduates, Carty enrolled in the required English course and walked into the classroom of Dr. James Glimm. Carty and Glimm shared an interest in music and history, and some of Glimm's stories stayed with Carty forever.

Dr. James Glimm, Professor of English, 1976.

"He went to school at the University of Texas and there was a mass shooting on campus. Back in those days, that was rare," remembers Carty. "He shared his experience with that, and I remembered it. He was my favorite professor; I connected with him."

While carrying a full credit course load each semester, Carty still managed to make time for sports. While at Mansfield, Carty played as an outside linebacker and a starter on the football team. "Sports consumed me," said Carty. "I also played baseball for just one year in college. The only reason for that was the coach didn't like people who played multiple sports." Carty wanted to play both sports and hoped that he could sway the opinion of the baseball coach. "He told me and another guy, 'you're both good enough for the team but he wouldn't be able to invite us back out until the [team] got back from their trip down south. It wouldn't be fair to them because you didn't play in the fall." This devastated Carty.

When not playing sports or studying, Carty found time for volunteerism. At the suggestion of one of his professors, Carty got involved with the local chapter of Big Brothers/Big Sisters. This was perhaps one of the first times where he got to work with children and strived

Mansfield Football Team, Fall 1977 (detail). Carty is #86.

to make a positive impact in a youngster's life. By 1978, Carty had all but completed his Bachelor's degree and had one more hurdle to jump over: student teaching. Placed at the nearby Williamson Junior and Senior High School, Carty got the opportunity to work with students in multiple grade levels as well as teach both American and world history. Looking back after so many decades, Carty remembers the only student problem during his placement happening on the very day that his professor from Mansfield was in the building to evaluate him! A student kept holding the classroom the door shut, preventing Carty from entering the room at the start of the class period. Eventually, Carty got the door open and pulled the kid out into the hallway and told him to stop it. Fortunately, neither the professor nor the sponsoring teacher took issue with how he handled the situation and Carty received a favorable evaluation.

Bachelor of Science in Education — Secondary Education

*Douglas L. Allen	*Shirley A. Eargle	Victor Koshuta
Wade E. Becker	†Beverly Ferguson	*Cindy L. Leister
Robert L. Carr	Michele L. Fuller	Nanette M. Litwin
Richard Carty	John K. Jones	Dennis J. Lomax
*Marie E. DeWitt	Patrick O. Kelley, Jr.	*Glen M. McNeal

Upper Left: *Carty's baccalaureate photo, 1978.*
Upper Right: *Williamson Junior-Senior High School.*
Bottom: *Excerpt from the 1978 Commencement Program.*

On May 20, 1978, Mansfield State College's annual commencement exercises began. Carty, along with twenty-three other graduates, earned the Bachelor of Science degree in secondary education. As he sat with the other four hundred degree candidates, he thought deeply about his future. "I remember being scared to death, thinking, 'what am I gonna do now?'"

The beginning of one's career can be compared to trying on clothing. The first garment tried on is not always a good fit, and that is okay. One's first job might not be the ideal position, but while moving around, one can expand their qualifications. For Carty, the first three years beyond the Baccalaureate degree contained some of the most insightful experiences of his life. Further, they were also some of the most unforgettable years.

Upon graduating from college, like many other college graduates, Carty needed a job. Little did he realize that his first job was not to teach, though it would involve young people. At the time, the Radio Corporation of America (RCA) owned a juvenile prison in Northampton, Pennsylvania, called Weaversville Intensive Treatment Unit. A childhood friend of Carty worked there and encouraged him to apply for a job. "The program director was a Vietnam vet, and my buddy from grade school was working there," said Carty. "I graduated in May and he said 'come work at Weaversville,' and I said okay."

Carty's first shift was on a Friday evening. Walking onto the grounds, he soon realized that this was going to be an intense experience. "My first night there, somebody took something from somebody else's room, and things got heated," Carty recalls. The staff who were on duty had a range of options for how to deal with teenagers fighting, but none of the options that crossed Carty's mind were even close to what happened that night. "The director says, 'get the gloves!'" A third staff member ran to a nearby closet and retrieved two sets of boxing gloves. "He yelled to the kids, 'you guys want to fight so much? Now, you're gonna fight! Three-minute rounds!'" He then had the rest of the nearby students form a circle around the two quarreling kids, so as not to let them get away from one another. "He let them punch each other for nine minutes. They were spent by the end of the first three minutes, but they had to fight for another six minutes. For as tough as they thought they were, they weren't tough." Thankfully, the rest of the evening was calm.

After spending the summer at Weaversville, Carty was ready for new opportunities and would once again receive his next opportunity through a telephone call. "A person who knew me from Easton was an assistant football coach at Lafayette College and had accepted a job on the coaching staff at Mansfield," said Carty. "I didn't know him but he knew me. He asked if I would be willing to sign on as an assistant football coach at Mansfield." The person was Joe Bottiglieri, who had recently been appointed as Mansfield's head coach. While the prospect of coaching excited Carty, he realized that this job did not pay enough. Not far from Mansfield was the Tioga County Detention Center, which was a maximum-security prison for juvenile delinquents. Given the experience of working at Weaversville, Carty decided to apply at Tioga County and was hired as a child care counselor. "My shift was from 6:30 a.m. until 2:30 p.m., and during football season, I'd go right from there to football practice." Much of Carty's coaching responsibilities revolved around scouting. "I had to do a lot of travel to scout opposing teams, and a lot of film breakdown. I didn't get to see many of our own games because of scouting," said Carty. Serving on the coaching staff at his alma mater was a very special experience and truly reinforced Carty's philosophy on teamwork, which he carried with him for the rest of his life.

If you can't throw, we just don't make you the quarterback. If you can't catch, we don't make you the receiver. If you can't run fast, we don't make you a running back. But there's a place for every one on that team, and if everyone is doing the best they can do and are pulling for one another, we're gonna have a good team.

As Carty witnessed the dedication of the Mansfield football players on the field, he also witnessed a very different kind of teenager at the Tioga County Detention Center. "They were probably there for everything but murder. That was lock up. They were adjudicated by the court system," said Carty. "In the morning, we went around, opened up their doors, and took them down to breakfast, and after breakfast, we taught."

In 1979, after a year of working at Tioga County, Carty decided to take a vacation to visit friends in Colorado. While there, he read a newspaper ad for a unique, but surprisingly fitting, opportunity.

VisionQuest, a privately run program for juvenile delinquents, was looking for staff members to facilitate their programs. [Note: VisionQuest should not be confused with the wilderness therapy programs for mental health issues or used as parental interventions. This program focused on teens youth sentenced via the criminal justice system, and was one of the first programs of its kind. Some of the methods would not be used today.]

A report for the Office of Juvenile Justice and Delinquency Prevention described their programs as follows:

> The impact programs operated by VisionQuest consisted of rustic wilderness camps, wagon trains pulled by horses and mules that traveled over the Western states, and extended sailing and bicycling expeditions. All of the programs emphasized physical conditioning, accountability for one's actions, and overcoming personal and physical challenges (quests). A youth would typically spend about three months in the wilderness camp, five months on a wagon train, and five months in a community residential program before being sent back to his home. In all of the VisionQuest programs, the staff reside with the program participants on a 24-hour basis.

Having worked with juvenile delinquents at both Weaversville and the Tioga County Detention Center, Carty was well-qualified for a position on the VisionQuest staff. He was hired and shown the ropes. "Staff members worked for six days, and then got two days off," said Carty. "The salary looked great, but on your two days off, they'd drop you off at the nearest town and you were responsible for paying for your hotel and meals. After you did that for two days, you were hardly making any money."

While Carty enjoyed the natural beauty of the rural western states, the experience was anything but relaxing. "You never slept more than six hours. The workday was divided into three shifts, and during all of those, the horses had to be fed and taken care of. I would spend three hours by the fire pit and feeding the horses."

The above description of this experience depicts a "best-case scenario," in that no unexpected issues arose. Oftentimes, the VisionQuest staff had to deal with behavioral problems. "One time, after a leave, I was instructed to take three kids and load up a horse trailer with firewood," Carty remembers. "In the middle of Colorado, kids would try to escape. After loading firewood, while we were waiting to be picked up, one kid said to me, 'what would you do if I ran right now?'"

The other kids paid close attention, wanting to see what Carty's response would be. "I told him, 'if you're gonna do it, now would be the best time for you to do it.' The kid said, 'you wouldn't run after me?' Nah, I'd stay here with the other two guys." Basically, I called his bluff." It was not uncommon for kids in the program to try and run away from the staff. "Kids would run, and sometimes they'd get fifty miles away, but they'd always get picked up and brought back." Upon returning to the group, the kids were punished, which included having to sleep by the fire and losing the comfort of riding in a wagon. "If you ran away, once you were caught and brought back, you walked for five days," said Carty.

After several months with VisionQuest, Carty grew tired of the strenuous pace of the position and decided to resign. Carty liked Colorado and wanted to stay there, but he could not find a permanent job. In December 1979, Carty flew back to the east coast and returned to his hometown of Easton, Pennsylvania. "Once I got home, I knew I wasn't going back out west," said Carty. He continued to search for jobs but had little luck. "People would tell me that I should do sales, so I gave that a shot," but soon realized that it wasn't a good fit.

Carty's niche was education, and that is where he belonged. In the early 1980s, finding a teaching position was very difficult, and Carty struggled. "I applied for a couple of jobs that were only open because somebody died," recalls Carty. So, like most beginning educators, Carty began substitute teaching. He covered classes in the Nazareth, East Stroudsburg, and Easton school districts. Eventually, a long-term substitute position became open at Easton as a junior high school social studies teacher. For almost a year, Carty taught a wide span of courses, ranging from geography to United States History. He even covered an industrial arts class for a month. "They liked me, and they said that a junior high job was going to open," said Carty. Unfortunately, this opportunity never materialized due to an unexpected drop in enrollment. "So, when somebody retired, they cut the junior high job and moved people around."

Carty's early years of teaching afforded him a wealth of experiences in education, however, what was missing was the steadiness of a permanent teaching position.

First Base
THE CAVALIER YEARS

In the early 1980s, the Pocono Mountain region was predominantly a vacation destination. Individuals and families throughout the tri-state area often traveled to the Poconos to enjoy its wealth of year-round outdoor activities. Honeymooners enjoyed the seclusion of its mountain-top resorts. Amid all of this, well-established towns carried out their nine-to-five lives and had rich traditions of school spirit and hometown pride. One of these towns, situated between the Delaware River and Brodhead Creek, was East Stroudsburg: a slice of suburbia, cradled in the wilderness.

North Courtland Street can be considered the spinal column of East Stroudsburg, spanning through residential and commercial properties. Along this route is East Stroudsburg High School, the public high school for several townships in both Monroe and Pike counties. The North Courtland Street property also housed the J.S. Bunnell School, which, by the early 1980s, was the East Stroudsburg Area School District's junior high school, housing grades seven and eight. On the other side of the property sat the administration center for the East Stroudsburg Area School District. While this complex was the focal point of the district's educational services, elementary-aged children attended schools at J.M. Hill, Smithfield, and Middle Smithfield Elementary schools.

The population was relatively small, with only 175 seniors graduating from the senior high school in 1981.

This small-town high school, overseen by East Stroudsburg State College graduate and long-time history teacher Charles Lehman, was a small but thriving community. The Cavaliers were offered a range of extra-curricular activities, including musical and dance groups to peer mediation caucuses. Like any high school, East Stroudsburg had its share of discipline problems among the student body.

East Stroudsburg Area Senior High School's front entrance.

In an effort to address these, the school instituted an internal suspension program around 1979. Douglas Arnold, an itinerant teacher in the district at the time, remembers this as "a necessary evil but it was a way to keep kids in school. If you kick them out, now what? That doesn't do people any good at all!" The "internal warden," as so affectionately titled in the 1981 yearbook, was Jim Wills. In addition to the responsibilities of the position which included reporting the school's daily attendance and supervising after-school detention, Wills coached basketball at nearby (what was then called)

From left to right: Charles Lehman ("keep it legal!"); Jim Wills.

East Stroudsburg State College. According to the yearbook, "he finds his job a challenge and he thinks the program works for most of the kids." Wills surprised the school body when he resigned in early February 1981, having accepted a teaching position in another district. The position for a replacement was posted, and Richard Carty came in for an interview. "It was a newish position and it involved dealing with some hard-core students," said Carty. "I had already dealt with juvenile delinquents in the past, and the district felt that I was qualified for the position. They were impressed with what I had done."

Motion was made by Mr. Smith and seconded by Mr. Turn to appoint Richard O. Carty Jr. In-School Suspension/Detention Supervisor effective February 23, 1981, for the remainder of the 1980-81 school year at a prorated annual salary of $10,112 for 7.5 hours per day, every day that school is in session for students. A replacement for James Wills who resigned. Motion carried. Voting in favor: Messrs. Smith, Turn, Sommer, Zaccaro, Featherman. Opposed: none. Tally: 5-yes; 0-no; 4-absent.

Minutes of the March 16, 1981 school board meeting, approving Carty's appointment.

On February 23, 1981, Carty was appointed as the In-School Suspension/Detention Supervisor. Meanwhile, Wills eventually went on to host televised sports programs on the Pennsylvania Cable Network (PCN). "I had not run across his path in all those years but I knew who he was," said Carty.

Despite the odd timing of his hiring, Carty quickly became known by nearly everyone in the building. His colleagues favored his demeanor in how he ran the Internal Suspension Program. "He ran it just like he ran anything else," recalled the school's athletic director Jim Reynolds. "He ran a tight ship. He didn't take a lot of guff from the kids. Nobody liked to go there at the time, and once they were there, they were there for a purpose, and that's the way it's gonna be." Despite the rigid nature of discipline, Carty was able to find the balance between being authoritative and treating students reasonably. "He was pretty low-key, he was pretty understanding, very patient and personable," Arnold remembers. "He respected the kids, and in turn, they respected him. He did a good job with that."

Reynolds and Arnold soon got to know Carty as even more than "the warden" when Carty decided to continue his tradition of coaching. At the time, East Stroudsburg's coaching staff was in a period of transition, particularly regarding football. Long-time head varsity football coach, Richard "Dick" Merring was stepping down, and assistant coach Ed Christian was taking the reigns as head coach for the 1981 season.

The 1981–82 Cavalier Varsity Football team. Carty is on the bottom right.

24

This left an opening in the staff, which Carty applied for and was selected. "He came in and he coached the tight ends and outside linebackers for years," said Arnold. "He was a good coach, there's no doubt about that. The players liked him and we had a very good staff at the time."

Carty was very impressed by his fellow coaching staff. "There were people that were there for a while," he recalls. "People stayed for a long time which is probably why the program was so good because they weren't going through changes every single year. All brilliant minds!" Carty quickly got to work with the outside linebackers, which was what he played while at Mansfield State College. Colleague Jeffrey Heard describes him as "a great football player in college. He went to Easton High School and he was a good player there too." As a coach, Carty believed in spelling out the expectations. "This is what I expect from you, and what you can expect from me. We covered everything," he said.

The baseball program at East Stroudsburg was also facing a transition in its coaching staff. Reynolds, who had coached the varsity baseball team for many years, relinquished his coaching responsibilities to replace Jack Kist as the athletic director. These personnel changes left both the head coach and assistant coach positions for the varsity baseball team vacant.

Carty had already started coaching football and was interested in coaching baseball as well. Frank Johnson, who was a physical education teacher at J.M. Hill Elementary School, recalls the hiring process. "We both applied for the same job as baseball coach," he recalls. "[Carty's] first year in the district, he applied for the head baseball coach job. I got it because I had more experience in the District."

At the December 14, 1981 meeting of the Board of Education, it was announced that Carty was named as the Assistant Varsity Baseball Coach. Johnson and Carty coached the varsity baseball team together for the next six years. When asked about his impressions of Carty, Johnson said that "he is the most sincere person I've ever met in education. He didn't wear his emotions on his sleeve, but he wore his sincerity on his sleeve."

The 1981–82 Cavalier Varsity Baseball team. Carty is in the second row, second from right.

"Frank was a good person. He was very organized and very regimented. I won't say that I was the most organized person in the world, but I learned a lot of organizational skills from him," said Carty. It was not long into his first year of coaching two sports when Carty earned a nickname: Rico. "We called him 'Rico' because there was a famous baseball player named Rico Carty at the time who played for the Braves," recalls Arnold. "When we heard the name 'Carty,' we automatically called him 'Rico.'" This nickname would be used by colleagues throughout the rest of Carty's career.

A coach's dedication and demeanor toward their players are rarely forgotten, even after many decades. Kelly Lewis, who graduated in 1982, played football and baseball at East Stroudsburg during Carty's first year on the coaching roster. "I walked on my senior year, which makes you kind of a unique player," Lewis recalls. "[Carty] took me under his wing, the 'scrub defense,' because right out of the gate I wasn't a starter. But through him I was able to start a couple of games." It was Lewis' senior year when Johnson and Carty's baseball coaching tenure began, which, to many seasoned players, can be problematic when two new coaches take over. Thankfully, it ended up being a positive situation, as Lewis recalls. "What I remember with Coach Carty was he communicated with students so well. Not too many teachers could connect with students so well. He didn't talk down to you." Of course, coaching does come with its share of negative experiences. An example of this is best explained by Carty himself:

> I was coaching football at the time. A kid who was injured and wasn't playing, apparently, while we were out at practice was going through lockers. He stole my ATM card, my bank was over in Stroudsburg, he went over and emptied out my account…and put the card back! I went there one day to make a withdrawal and the teller said "you don't have any money in this account." I hadn't used the account yet. I went in the bank and said "when did I supposedly take this out?" She gave me the time and date. Then I asked if there was anyone else who had taken anything else right before or right after that. Today, they wouldn't give you that information. She gave me the person's name who made a withdrawal right after this particular withdrawal happened, and as luck would have it, I actually knew this person. So, I called them up and asked them who was in front of them when they went to the bank. One thing after another, I narrowed it down. I went to Charlie Lehman and he brought the kid in. The kid confessed.

Carty spent many hours on the football and baseball fields each week, watching the players make sacrifices and dedicate themselves to achieving excellence. Coaching was not Carty's only contribution to the school. After finishing his first semester on the faculty, the administration needed teachers to teach summer school. Nobody stepped forward to teach physical education, so Carty stepped up to the plate. By September of 1982, Carty was considered a first-year probationary teacher while still tasked with oversight of the Internal Suspension program.

Carty soon became known to students as more than a disciplinarian when he established "The Social Club." This group was open to all students. Membership was based on nomination and selected by the office staff. The Club, as described in the 1985 yearbook, "receives a catered luncheon at which time Mr. Carty steps aside to welcome a guest speaker." Field trips were also a part of The Social Club, and "Mr. Carty usually invites a female faculty member to accompany the group on such trips."

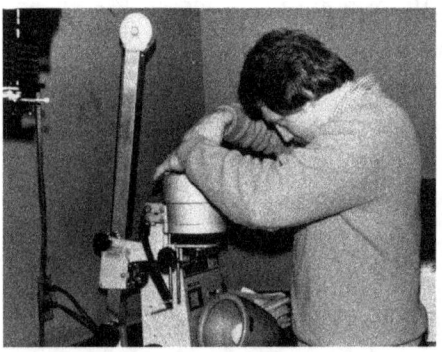

Carty Heads Social Club.

Every day the East Stroudsburg Social Club and Fun Bunch meets with club director Mr. Carty. Although membership is open to any and all students, only a select few attend the meetings on a regular basis.

"We love getting new members," explained Mr. Carty. "We don't want to create an elitist image for ourselves." Most nominations for admission into the social club come from faculty or staff, but the office makes the final membership appointments.

During the day the club receives a catered luncheon at which time Mr. Carty steps aside to welcome a guest speaker. Two field trips also highlight the day. Mr. Carty usually invites a female faculty member to accompany the group on such trips.

Most of the time, however, the club members practice their meditation techniques. "It's a very relaxing atmosphere," reported one Social Clubber who was no doubt too proud to reveal his identity. "I've only been selected for a two day tour this year, but I hope to improve my record next fall.

Clockwise: Carty setting up a photo enlarger; a write-up about The Social Club printed in the yearbook; Carty in the internal suspension room, 1985.

28

Around the same time in the mid-1980s, Carty put his photography training to use for the production of the school yearbook. In the words of the yearbook staff, "Rick Carty… took pictures, and set up and taught students to develop and enlarge photos when the staff was in desperate need."

Like most teachers, Carty often found himself in the faculty room during his lunch period. It was here where he got to know his colleagues on an informal basis and even got to have some fun with them. As lunch period draws to a close, a common wish is for someone else to make the long walk back to the cafeteria with their tray. The East Stroudsburg faculty found a perfect solution for this by instituting "Flip Score." "That was part of our entertainment for the day," Carty explains. "We'd flip a coin and whoever lost had to carry the trays back." Records were kept of the winnings and losses, and at the end of the school year, the person who lost the most won "The Golden Tray Award," which was a cafeteria tray that was painted gold. "It wasn't my idea, but I was in on it," Carty admits.

"Gentlemen Prepare Your Quarters"

A casual observer in the first lunch period would note a flurry of activity as the period draws to a close. A large group gathers around the commissioners, and with quarters or other coins in hand, they proceed to flip coins in the first round of play. Those that are disqualified, heave a sigh of relief while the tension mounts for the second round flippers. When all is said and done, one poor soul, "the winner", gets his or her name added to the official scoreboard and has to carry out everyone's lunch trays. The "winner" or "loser" it appears, is no garbage man and what is a most amazing phenomena is that the "guest" flipper always seems to lose.

FLIPSCORE	
DENNIS	1
RICO	2
KEG	2
LARRY	1
BRAD	1
DICK	1 ·
MARK	1
GLEN	0
SUE	0
JIM	1
GUEST	1
·RECORD	10

Even students took an interest in the daily "flipscore," as shown in the yearbook.

Carty enjoys a lively lunch period with his colleagues, spring 1984.

While sitting around the table in the faculty room, Carty listened to his colleagues talk, which often included gossip and complaining. "People would say, 'this is really wrong!' about something or other, and my thought was, if you think you can do better, go do it. I felt I could do better."

This epiphany motivated Carty to enroll at East Stroudsburg University's graduate program in Secondary Education. Between the convenient location, their long-time commitment to teacher education, and the already strong ties with the district, ESU seemed the perfect place for Carty to study. Beginning in June of 1984, Carty began taking graduate courses in secondary education every summer for the next five years. These included Introduction to Research, Mainstreaming in the Schools, The Learner and Learning Process, and Educational Administration, among others. ESU's Department of Professional and Secondary Education offered certification tracks for those interested in teaching as well as for those seeking principal certification. Among Carty's professors were Donald Bortz, who had earlier served as a principal in the Nazareth School District. Carty earned a Letter of Equivalency for a Master's Degree, or "MEQ," from the Pennsylvania Department of Education in September of 1989. On May 19, 1990, Carty was conferred the Master of Education degree in Secondary Education alongside six other candidates for this degree.

East Stroudsburg University's 1990 Commencement Program cover.

As Carty pursued his graduate studies, he continued to coach football and baseball. During his tenure as assistant coach of the varsity football team, the Cavaliers quickly developed a strong reputation throughout northeastern Pennsylvania. In his second year on the coaching staff, the Cavaliers scored an 8-3 record and won the Centennial League Championship. Two years later, the Cavaliers once again earned this honor, but unfortunately the odds were against them. The fall 1984 season began with very few experienced players on the roster, and the team was described by many as "rebuilding." According to the yearbook, "With hard work and determination, these students put together one of the finest Cavalier football teams in recent history." This statement is evidenced by a string of eight victories." The 1985 season saw an impressive record of eleven wins, one loss as well as winning the District Championship over Palmerton High School, with a whopping score of 34-0. "They inducted that team into the Hall of Fame because they were the first team that won a district championship," recalls Carty. All in all, Carty's years as an assistant football coach were successful and rewarding. "I learned a lot from all of them," said Carty. "It was a lot of fun and we won a lot of games and a lot of championships."

The 1985 Varsity Football team. Carty is seated in the top row, third from left.

As each football season came to a close, a new baseball season was at its dawn. The spring 1982 season, which was Carty's first, could be described as average. While eight wins, nine losses, and a tie is not the ideal score tally for any coach, the season was not without success. The Cavaliers competed and won against each Centennial League component, barring the year's champion, Pocono Mountain High School. Additionally, two of the players, John Seneca and Ed Facyson, were named to the Centennial League's All-League Second Team. Throughout the 1980s, Carty continued to coach the varsity baseball team alongside Frank Johnson. "He's always been a really good team player, and that's why we did well together. We were there for the kids and there to make sure they are successful," recalls Johnson.

Coaching two sports while pursuing a Master's degree was very time-consuming for Carty. After six successful seasons, Johnson decided to step down as head varsity baseball coach. In October 1987, it was announced that Carty would become the head baseball coach for the varsity team for the 1988 season. Working with Kevin Kuchinski, a physical education teacher and assistant varsity coach, this new coaching regime realized that fun was a key ingredient for success.

"I asked myself," Carty remembers, "'what do I have to do to make this successful?' I have to make it fun for these kids, and that's what I did. I made it fun for them to be at practice and, in the end, we worked on fundamentals and we had some good teams. And we won!"

Above: The 1988 Cavalier Varsity
Baseball Team
Right: Carty as head coach

There were, however, challenges to be addressed by the coaches. Carty, reflecting on his first season as the head baseball coach:

My first year was a little rocky. Four seniors quit. They felt because they were seniors that it was their turn to play, but I didn't see things that way. I felt that the best guys play, it doesn't matter if they're a sophomore, a junior, or a senior, if you're better than the next guy, you're gonna play. Our goal is to go out, compete, and win. At the end of the season, I only had eleven kids left. We started with fifteen and four seniors quit.

Upon placing in districts, Carty recommended to Kuchinski that they promote a few students from the junior varsity team to the varsity team. While he knew that these rookie players would likely not play in any games, at least the Cavaliers would look like a full team. Kuchinski agreed. "They were thrilled to be up there on the varsity team, just practicing and being on the bench at a district game," said Carty. When interviewed by *The Morning Call* newspaper, Carty assured that "regardless of what happens, we still play for the championship at the end and these guys will do well."

Indeed, they did well, as the Cavaliers took home the 1988 Centennial League Championship after winning against Notre Dame of Green Pond. This was the first time that East Stroudsburg had won this honor since 1955, which, ironically, was the year that Carty was born. One year later, Carty's players earned a second victory when the Cavaliers beat Dieruff 13-6, and in doing so, broke down the "perceived superiority" felt by teams in the East Penn Conference. Carty shared his thoughts on this with *The Morning Call*:

Hey, we put our cleats on the same way they do; and we buy our bats from the same company. I kept telling the kids we'd have to come out swinging the way we did all year. Were they confident? Absolutely. We told them all week they could play with anyone. And they believe that. We needed a game like this to get the blood boiling.

The 1989 season was a very successful run for the Cavaliers, having won eighteen games and only losing three. Unfortunately, the season ended with a loss, but like any good coach, Carty reflected on the game honestly and pointed out the weak spots:

We made too many errors. We hit the ball just as well as they did, I thought, but we didn't make the plays and they did. It's a shame, too, because we're capable of playing some pretty good defense. And we have — but not tonight.

Upon becoming the head coach, Carty was able to further develop his leadership skills and manage the team his own way. "When I was the assistant coach, if one person did something wrong, everybody had to run. Then the other guys hated the one guy who did it. I did change that when I became in charge. I would not do a blanket consequence to the whole team when one person did something wrong," said Carty. "He was one of the coaches that took care of his problems," said Jim Reynolds. "When a parent had a problem, he'd sit down and talk with them, reason with them, and some coaches would enflame that situation and then it would come to my desk. Most of the time Rico handled his problems and did a good job with them."

Another eyewitness to Carty's coaching style was Jeffrey Heard, who coached the junior varsity team for one year before replacing Kuchinski as varsity assistant coach in 1990.

Rico is a very honest person. Very fair, always explaining to the players and to the students what they are doing well, what they can improve on, and why. And never any secrets. Never anyone being left out. He believed in communicating, believed in keeping everyone in the loop. Being firm and fair. He'd give you the same amount of time if you were the best player or best student or someone that struggled. I love that, I respect that, and that's how it should be.

Heard and Carty's first season coaching together went well, but this collaboration was soon interrupted by world events. Heard, who was in the United States Army Reserves, was called to duty in the Gulf War. In his absence, former Cavalier player Steve Schuppe was selected as an interim assistant coach. "We had a young team and we just kept teaching and I know he was impressed," said Carty. "He marveled at how we grew and kids learned and got better. I was patient and didn't get upset with what they were doing. We just kept working to get better." The 1991 baseball season's record was 7 wins,

Top: The 1990 Varsity Baseball Team
Above: Jeffrey Heard

11 losses, though the Cavaliers won five out of their last six games. "I was very proud of that team. I was as proud of them as I was of the kids who won two back-to-back titles," said Carty.

The year 1992 was a year of change for Carty. In May of that year, after eleven seasons, three league titles and one district title victory,

Carty decided to stop coaching football, effective immediately. "I needed to take something off my plate since I was also coaching baseball," he said.

The 1992 Cavalier Golf Team

One of Carty's favorite pastimes was playing golf, though he never considered the idea of coaching a golf team before. To his surprise, the opportunity presented itself in 1992 when the head golf coach resigned. On August 17, 1992, the school board approved Carty as the head golf coach, however, not without mixed opinions. An eyewitness at a board meeting, who declined to comment on the record, observed several board members saying "that's just great, that's just what we need...a football mentality coaching golf!" While initially offended by this remark, Carty soon reinterpreted it as motivation to win. "I think golf was a better fit for him," says Arnold. "A little less stress, a little more opportunity to coach baseball, and he loved golf to begin with, and loved to work with kids." At the time, the Cavalier golfers practiced at The Mountain Manor Resort, located just several miles north of the high school in Marshalls Creek. "When Rico first started as the golf coach, we were playing golf there and they didn't charge us a nickel!" says Reynolds.

Walking into the first practice of the season, Carty knew he had his work cut out for him. "The first thing I did was restore order and discipline, which they didn't have prior to me getting there." Unfortunately, Carty was met with a few seniors who did not take well to such a coaching style. To their disappointment, they were removed from the team. "That probably got everybody else's attention and they showed up and walked the line," Carty said. Carty's first season as the golf coach was highly successful, finishing with a 13-3 record and having three players advance to districts. "It just so happened that we had some kids who could really play golf. I told them, 'if you come here, show up, and do what I ask you to do, I think we could win it all!'" Carty told his players.

Under Carty's leadership, the team won first and second place positions in the Centennial League Tournament. Moreover, two players placed for the District Qualifying Tournament, and later, advanced to the District Tournament. The players, some of whom had been on the team for several years, spoke highly of their new coach. "Coach Carty gave the team a lot of motivation," said 1993 graduate Howie VanBuskirk. One concern, which all coaches face time and again, was the loss of several graduating seniors.

Thankfully, despite losing several key players to graduation, the 1993 season was not only victorious but record-breaking. One player, Jason Dreisbach, placed in both the District and State tournaments. "Jason was the first qualifier in East Burg in eight years," Carty said to the yearbook staff. "He also won the Centennial League Tournament with a score of 73." The school's golf record, which had been held for eighteen years, was finally broken.

When reflecting on his second season as coach, Carty said that "we knew that we were a young team hoping to play well. We finished on a positive note. I think depth was our main strength. We are a young, experienced team...[and] our goal is to win a league title next year."

Richard Carty, 1993

After his first year of coaching golf, Carty desired to learn more about coaching golf and the sport itself. In the summer of 1993, the Ladies Professional Golf Association (LPGA) held a week-long class in coaching golf.

Carty signed up and traveled to Williamsburg, Virginia to attend the class, which was facilitated by retired college golf coaches. From nine to five, Carty was either in a classroom or on the golf range. "I got a golf teaching certificate from it and I'd felt like I learned a lot," Carty said.

The 1993 golf season was equally successful as the prior year. Carty, who was prouder than ever of his young team, preached the value of consistency while instilling a strong team spirit. When interviewed by the yearbook staff, Dreisbach, who had been twice named "most valuable player," commented that "the team is more important than individual playing."

Once again, the Cavaliers placed in the district tournament. In 1995, the team won the newly established Mountain Valley Conference Title. The team won the Centennial League Tournament Title in 1995 and again in 1996.

Above: The 1995 Cavalier Golf Team
Right: The team celebrating a win at DiVilla's Pizzeria, 1996

As the players practiced four afternoons each week, one aspect of the sport that Carty instilled in his team was that "golf is a different natured sport in that the players have to carry themselves well and always display good sportsmanship." Good sportsmanship is necessary, especially in a situation where your team is comprised of inexperienced players.

The graduating class of 1997 saw nearly the entire team leave, resulting in Carty having to rebuild his winning team. "The team is young and inexperienced," said Carty to the yearbook staff, "but however, not being denied of any fun. We're improving, learning a lot, and handling each match better and better." The 1997 season was not as successful as years past, but the Cavaliers managed to earn third place in the Mountain Valley Conference League Championship.

"Golf is more of a white-collar sport, kinda like tennis," Carty said. "We didn't really have a lot of white-collar kids to begin with. These kids from East Stroudsburg, they weren't 'country club kids.' You go to some of the richer school districts, those kids that are playing golf, their parents usually have money. They grew up around country clubs. That's not what I had."

Carty's colleagues praise his work as a golf coach. "He had some kids go on to play at the advanced level and a couple of them are now in the golf course management business, some of them here in the Poconos and some of them elsewhere," said Reynolds. Additionally, Carty was a strong proponent of a coeducational team.

"I would really like to see the girls coming out for golf," he said. "I've seen some of these girls play, and they can really play!…We did what we had to do, and in the process, we had a lot of fun…and, we won! It was a good time of my life." Clearly, Carty's lessons in good sportsmanship paid off.

Nearly any educator who taught during the 1980s and '90s was likely exposed to rapid developments in technology. The East Stroudsburg Area School District's faculty and administrators were no exception to this, though the presence of technology was already a large part of the District's operations.

From as far back as the late 1970s, the District had contracted with (then) East Stroudsburg State College for support with data processing. In 1979, the District installed its first mainframe computer, an IBM machine that ran HGA software titled "Application System 400." The "AS-400," as it was nicknamed by District employees, was located in the North Courtland School and included two applications.

The first application, known as "Student Sphere," was used for student scheduling, attendance, and transportation records. The second, known as "Accusphere," was used for the business functions of the District, such as accounting and payroll. For many years, each school had a terminal in the office, and the buildings were connected through a dial-up connection. Generally speaking, students had nothing to do with the administrative computing systems, however, computers had become a part of the academic program as early as the 1980s.

Thanks to the foresight of the faculty in the Mathematics Department, in 1982, six TRS-80 Model 3 computers were purchased and integrated into both statistics courses and computer programming. By 1985, an introductory course in computer literacy was developed, and by 1990, the District's elementary schools were integrating computers into the curriculum through coursework and extra-curricular activities. "Computers to me, was like Greek," Carty admits.

Change is inevitable, and within a school district, it is ever-present and multi-faceted. One change that is often most visible to the staff is when new leadership takes over. In 1985, during Carty's fifth year in the district, the principal, Charles Lehman, resigned to accept a position as the personnel director at Skytop Lodge.

Succeeding Lehman was Ronald Meyer, who was a 1966 graduate of East Stroudsburg. After less than two years, Meyer left and was replaced by James Bonner. A characteristic of Bonner's eight years as principal, and certainly of his successors, is population growth.

The Pocono Mountain region was quickly growing during the 1980s. According to *The Morning Call* newspaper, East Stroudsburg Area School District's enrollment in 1983 was 1,072. By 1989, it had grown by 477 students, or 44%. This growth made it clear that more facilities were needed, particularly in the high school. Plans were made for a $5 million addition, which included a new library, auxiliary gymnasium, eight new classrooms, and various renovations.

The opening of this new facility was not the only ceremonious occasion to take place on campus in early 1990. The playing fields located on the high school property were named "The Gersham H. Litts Fields," named for a local contractor who was a great supporter of the Cavalier sports teams.

Growth and expansion became a major theme of the 1990s. Relocatable classrooms, commonly referenced as "modulars" or "pods," were being installed at nearly every school site within the district. Classes were crowded. Bill David, who was a newly-hired science teacher in 1991, recalls this period of growth:

> The growth was unbelievable, exponential! By the time I got to be a senior in college in 1991, and I did my student teaching at East Stroudsburg, they were bursting at the seams at that time and were already overcrowded. They were looking for different ways to expand and meet the needs of the growing community.

Enrollment continued to soar, with 355 new students entering the district in 1991. According to the meeting minutes of the Board of Education, "it does not appear that the enrollment growth is slowing down."

Unfortunately, relocatable classrooms were only a temporary solution. While these spaces offered more places for teaching, they did not fix the problem of travel time to and from school, nor the problem of overcrowding in common areas. Hallways, cafeterias, locker rooms, and athletic facilities were in need of relief, too.

This strain was felt not only in the high school but in the junior high school. Discussion of building a new intermediate school began in the mid-1980s to no avail. Finally, in January 1991, ground was broken on a new intermediate school.

Photos on opposite page:
Top: Ronald Meyer (Principal 1985–87) and Dr. James Bonner (1987–95)
Center: The back of the high school in the 1980s, prior to the new library addition
Bottom: Class being held in a modular classroom during the 1980s

This new building would relocate the seventh- and eighth-grade students from the aging J. S. Bunnell school as well as the sixth-graders in the North Courtland Elementary School to a new facility on Route 209. Because of the merging of grades six through eight in one building, the new school would not be a junior high school but instead an intermediate school.

J.S. Bunnell Building

J.T. Lambert Intermediate School, opened in 1992

The new intermediate school, named in honor of the retiring superintendent John T. Lambert, opened in September of 1992. To help minimize the large size of the school, the J.T.L. school utilized a cohort system with interdisciplinary "teams" of teachers who instructed a select portion of a particular grade level. The Bunnell building, which was situated next to the high school, now became part of the high school complex. Numerous classes, including home economics, photography, and many of the ninth-grade core classes were moved into the Bunnell building. The principal, James Bonner, decided to relocate the internal suspension room to the basement of the Bunnell building. "They would use a couple of rooms in the basement of the Bunnell as classrooms," recalled Robert Green, who was a shop teacher at the high school. "It was kind of a maze to get down there!" Carty worked out of this location for the next five years. "The I.S.S. room was relocated three or four times while I was there," said Carty.

With growth comes change, not only in terms of facilities but the mindsets of the inhabitants. A long-standing tradition at East Stroudsburg High School's commencement ceremonies was to have a benediction, a prayer, as part of the ceremony. In May of 1992, several students went to the Board of Education and requested that this be removed from the program. The meeting minutes cite the request as such: "…The ethnic and cultural diversity of the class means that all students do not recognize the same God." With a petition of nearly eighty signatures and the pending ruling of *Lee v. Weisman* at the Supreme Court, the Board agreed to remove the prayer from commencement.

Diversity continued to be a focal point for the District. In January of 1994, the district offered a staff development program titled "Are our students prepared to live in a multicultural society?" The cultural flavor of the Pocono region only continued to diversify in the years ahead.

From the viewpoint of students, many of the topics discussed by the Board are not very obvious. To any student who attended East Stroudsburg High School between 1994 and 1996, two changes occurred that were undoubtedly more noticeable. The first change was toward "intensive scheduling," which utilized blocks instead of the nine-period timetable used in the past. A social studies teacher, Kevin Nace, recalled this change:

> Block scheduling was implemented as a huge cost saving measure for the district (mostly based on staff usage). At the time, we had a nine-period day and teachers taught five classes and covered one duty (study hall, lunch, etcetera). When we switched to four blocks, each teacher taught three blocks of the day, which is the same as teaching six classes in a traditional schedule.

While Carty was not a fan of this new scheduling model, this change saw tangible benefits, such as only needing half the number of text-books, and the ability to hire study hall or cafeteria monitors at a cheaper wage. There were drawbacks, of course. Robert Green expressed his perspective on this new schedule:

> Believe it or not, in the shop classes, the kids were more productive when they had periods rather than blocks. You'd think having double the time would make them more productive but they weren't. In a class where you're producing things, materials have to dry, and if kids at the beginning of class glued their stuff together, what do they do for the next hour? You had to come up with remedies for that. When they were there for 45 minutes, they got their project glued together in the half hour they had. When they came in the next day, bang! It was ready. They weren't sitting around waiting for glue to dry...literally.

The second change that took place in 1995, which was perhaps even more noticeable, was the resignation of the principal, James Bonner. Chosen as his successor was Michael Michaels, a new hire for the district who brought experience in elementary and special education with him. It was during Michaels' tenure as principal where the East Stroudsburg Area School District saw some of the most drastic growth and change. MaryGrace Anderson, née McDowell, an art teacher and a 1990 graduate of the High School, reflects on this growth:

> The population had exploded. There were a lot more kids at the high school, and even with the new addition, it seemed like they needed more space. I had friends that would travel forty-five minutes on a bus. You had the people who were in town and the people who were traveling really far.

With growth in population comes the need for more administrators. The 1990s saw several individuals wearing the assistant principal hat, including business education teacher Margaret DiNardo; a new hire from the Pleasant Valley School District Irene Duggins; and Anthony Crimaldi, who, similarly to Carty, began his career certified in social studies and later pursued an administrative position.

Michael Michaels (Principal 1995–99) and Anthony Crimaldi

By the summer of 1996, Carty had been enrolled in graduate courses at East Stroudsburg University for four additional semesters beyond his Master's degree. Among the courses he took was a graduate-level course titled "Computers in Education," as he was well aware of the technological skill set he would need in the years ahead. "I was forced to learn about computers. I needed to know this stuff because scheduling and all that stuff was on computers. I wasn't savvy with that but I needed to learn." Carty vividly recalls his first day in the computer course:

> I get in this class, and I was to the point where I was so afraid to touch buttons. I had that phobia that if I touch it, it might blow up. There's about twenty people in this class, and the professor tells us to start doing the activity. And my computer is not working, or I don't know what the hell I'm doing, and everybody else is moving ahead. I call the professor over, he says, "this computer is not working right," and I'm thinking "my luck," as I'm trying to learn this stuff and get started out. By the time he moved me to another spot, everyone was ten minutes ahead of me on the assignment, and that just turned me off. I did what I had to do to learn how to use it, but I'm not a big computer person.

In his fifteen years at East Stroudsburg, Carty had not only seen tremendous changes, but also tremendous growth. The senior class of 1981 was comprised of 175 students, and by 1996, that number had grown to 244 students, according to the yearbooks. Interestingly, Carty never opted to transition into the social studies department. "The In-School Suspension program was running pretty smoothly. I thought, there isn't really any need for me to jump over to the classroom unless something opened up. In the meantime, I started going back to school for my administrative certification," said Carty.

With change also comes departure, and in late fall 1997, assistant principal Anthony Crimaldi resigned from his position. Carty's aspiration of working in administration was still strong, and with the blessing of his supervisors, he applied for the position. While going through the interview process, Carty was asked a question that he will never forget. "One of the people interviewing me asked, 'how will you discipline the Black students?' I thought to myself, 'What? Is this a trick question?' So, I answered, 'simple. I don't discipline color; I discipline right and wrong.' It must have been the right answer. That's exactly how I felt and I learned that from the two coaches I had in high school who happened to be Black. They never treated anybody differently because they were Black or weren't Black. They treated everybody based on right and wrong."

In December of 1997, Carty began his administrative tenure as assistant principal and head of discipline. His philosophy on administration can be summarized in just three words: "discipline with dignity." Similar to his coaching style, Carty believed in showing respect to students, even in situations where punitive measures needed to be taken.

Students and faculty alike recall his demeanor as approachable and respectful. "People don't have to always like what you have to say," says Jeff Heard, "but if they know you're telling the truth, they respect it, and being an assistant principal, sometimes you have to tell people things that they don't want to hear. But I'm pretty sure the majority of the students respected what Rico had to say and respected him as a person. "I didn't put a wall up between myself and students," said Carty, "and I never put a wall up between myself and the staff members. A lot of times, people get into administration and it becomes us versus them. In my mind, that's not how it should be. Everybody matters."

Carty's philosophy of treating students with respect and ensuring a team-like atmosphere within the school can be attributed to the leadership he observed from Alfredean Jones and William Houston while growing up in Easton.

Race meant nothing to Carty. Unfortunately, when others brought race into the discussion, it stung, and as an administrator, it is likely to be brought up at some point or another. While serving as assistant principal, Carty had to suspend a Black student for a disciplinary infraction, following the usual protocol. The next day, the student's parent came into Carty's office. After Carty explained why the student had been suspended, the parent grew angrier and angrier. "She said to me, 'the only reason you suspended my kid is because he's Black.'" Carty became enraged. "I said 'first of all, I'm highly offended that you'd say that to me. You don't even know me! If that's what you think, you need to get out of my office right now!'" Carty's anger did not come from defensiveness, but rather, from the fact that his two dearest mentors were Black and taught him not to look at color. Thankfully, the situation did not escalate further, and Carty was never again accused of racism.

While serving as assistant principal, Carty was encouraged to consider "creative" approaches to discipline. Clearly, the common practice of assigning detentions was not proving to be effective. What is an administrator to do when they finally catch the student who makes a daily habit of throwing a chocolate milk carton at the wall? "They sent him to me, and I called his mother," Carty recalls. "I said to her, 'with your permission, I'm not gonna suspend him from school, but what I'd like to do is have him work with the custodians for two hours every morning before school. After all, we had to clean up his mess!'" The mother agreed, and the student spent a week helping the morning custodial staff. "Once his week was up, he wanted to keep doing it! People noticed him and he liked the attention," said Carty.

It was not long before Carty assumed the role of mentor to another aspiring administrator when Bill David, who had been serving as the Science Department chair, was appointed as the school's assistant disciplinarian.

Bill David, Assistant Disciplinarian

In this role, David worked closely with Carty, as he recalls:

> [Carty] was a fantastic mentor. He really showed me how to care about kids and understand where kids are coming from. He was consistent, he was firm, but he was also caring, and the students reacted to that demeanor of his. He's the kind of guy that draws you to him. His personality is magnetic. He really got kids, and that was something that really rubbed off on me.

With David handling much of the discipline functions, Carty was able to get involved in other aspects of school administration, ranging from the routine functions to the pressing issues. One aspect of the job was the submission of grades for report cards. In the 1990s, submitting grades was a cumbersome process in which faculty members had to pencil all student grades onto computer response forms. Then, Carty needed to review each form and ensuring that it was filled in properly. Trish Leibig, née Kaszupski, remembers "a long line at the office of teachers wanting to hand in their grade sheets. Mr. Carty had to verify all the grade sheets on the last day of school. We couldn't leave the building until he signed off on them!"

The management of a school requires knowledge of the resources and infrastructures that shape how it runs. The district's utilization of technology was quickly increasing during the latter half of the 1990s.

In quick succession, classrooms were all equipped with telephones and direct-dial extensions, replacing the intercom systems which only permitted calls to and from the main office. Soon after, select classrooms were equipped with dial-up Internet connections. In 1998, the District's first website, under the domain name "CavalierNet," was created through a partnership with East Stroudsburg University's Computer Science program. New coursework in aviation, multimedia and computer graphics became popular electives in the high school. The integration of email soon followed which is considered by some to be one of the technological marvels that forever shaped the American workplace.

The first version of "CavalierNet," the school's Web site, as it appeared in 1998.

Carty was all the wiser about email, and advised his staff about how it should be used.

> People can say things or write things that they normally wouldn't do if they were sitting in front of the person. That's what I used to always tell the teachers. When they had complaints from parents sent in emails, I said "Don't respond to that. Call them, get them in front of you. They'll rarely be as mean to you sitting in front of you as they can be behind a computer screen." That was my advice to them. Don't get involved in word wars and battles. Get them in your classroom and have a meeting with them. It will go a lot better than playing that game on the computer.

School principals must be prepared to deal with the unexpected, however serious or dangerous the scenario may be. Of course, even the most astute leader was likely shaken up on April 20, 1999, when Columbine High School in Colorado endured a shooting and attempted bombing. The response across the country was that of shock and fear, and even though East Stroudsburg High School was thousands of miles away from Columbine, the school community was affected by the tragedy. "It was very bone-chilling to go back to school the next day," recalls Debra Padavano, who was a paraprofessional at the high school. "Your guard's down, you're doing things, and then all of the sudden, something happens and your whole outlook changes." "It was a very shocking thing that made everyone aware that this could happen," said Green. "A lot of training took place after that and you had to be really mindful of security," said Carty. "It really changed how you look at security."

The end of the school year is always marked by the celebration of the graduating class. Parents look forward to seeing their child cross the stage. Students approach the day with bittersweet feelings. Administrators prepare for what *could* happen on this day. Principal Michael Michaels placed Carty in charge of planning the commencement ceremony. "Graduating classes would try to outdo the other with ridiculous pranks," Carty said.

East Stroudsburg Area Senior High School

EAST STROUDSBURG, PENNSYLVANIA

The One Hundred Ninth Commencement

FRIDAY, JUNE SIXTEENTH
TWO THOUSAND
Memorial Stadium
Seven o'clock in the evening

With a rising student population, seating at the commencement ceremonies became a problem. Wanting to remedy this, Carty suggested that graduation be held at East Stroudsburg University's Koehler Fieldhouse, a large, indoor venue that could afford each graduate several tickets for family members. "People went nuts!" he recalled. Nobody wanted the graduation to be held off campus, and the administration obliged.

On the morning of graduation day, sure enough, the Cavalier stadium was rained on. The high school gymnasium could only hold so many people, which meant that security could only let so many people into the building. People were angry and became hostile with the security guards. One guard asked Carty, "what should I tell these people?" Carty's response, "Ask them, 'who's seat would you like me to remove who was here before you?'" How could one argue that?

Eventually, the community's dissatisfaction with the limited seating at graduation reached the airwaves. Several days after graduation, Carty tuned in to the local radio station, 93.5 WSBG, where East Stroudsburg High School was the talk of the morning. Parents of graduates were calling into the morning show, venting their frustrations and attacking the school administration. Wanting to set the record straight, Carty called the radio station. "I identified myself and explained to the host that those parents were given the opportunity to hold graduation at a larger venue, that would have allowed each student to receive more tickets, and they turned it down." Shortly after, the conversation of the morning show shifted to other topics.

By the end of the twentieth century, Carty had achieved his goal of becoming an administrator. He had the unique experience of serving as assistant principal during a period of cultural diversification and technological innovation. Carty completed a graduate degree and became a respected, reliable presence at East Stroudsburg High School. Carty continued to coach two sports each year.

With change comes sacrifice. For Carty, this presented itself quite drastically in November of 1998 when the School Board voted against administrators coaching sports. When interviewed by *The Pocono Record* in March of 1999, Carty admitted that he "[is] going to miss just being out there, being able to work with the kids. I looked forward to coaching kids who are excited about being there." Jim Reynolds recalls this decision as having "a little bit of controversy because while he was an assistant principal, they allowed him to coach for the first year. And after the first year was over, they told him he couldn't coach anymore if he was going to be an administrator." Though this new policy saddened Carty, he realized the reality of the situation. As Carty explained to *The Pocono Record*:

It's one of those things. You want to move up the ladder in terms of your career, but you love coaching. You can't do both. You would think that some people, after 17 years, they'd had enough, but I can honestly say that I really wasn't ready to go.

Jeff Heard, who succeeded Carty as the head coach of the varsity baseball team, recalls this being a tough situation at the time.

I really enjoyed working with Rico, being a part of his staff. I would've been an assistant coach of his forever because, just like he treated the players, that's how he treated the coaches. He gave us a job to do, he trusted that we would do it, and then we would talk about it, evaluate how he thought we were doing. He was always open and fair. It wasn't just a loss for him, it was a loss for the district because we had to replace someone who was very successful.

Carty's final coaching season was the fall 1998 golf season. To some, the season could be looked at as disappointing in comparison with the successes of prior years. According to the yearbook, the Cavaliers only won two of its fifteen matches and placed 1-10 in the Mountain Valley Conference. "It was a rough year," said Carty, "however we had a great time. We made a good run at it in the end. The team has a lot of talent. However, we all must make fun a priority to succeed in this year's new conference."

While the end of a coaching career often comes with a feeling of closing the door on a major life chapter, a much bigger door was soon to open in Carty's life.

Second Base
THE TIMBERWOLF YEARS

On a late autumn night in the year 2000, a group of East Stroudsburg students wrote an alma mater song that began, "Deep within the forest green, nature's wonders hide, rays of sunlight can be seen reflecting our school pride." These lyrics were not a rewrite of Marjorie Slider's "The Purple and the White," but rather, a new chapter in East Stroudsburg's history. This new chapter took place within the Delaware State Forest of Pike County, on a new campus, that would quickly develop its own traditions, identity, and culture. It also signified a major turning point in Richard Carty's career, the opening of East Stroudsburg's North Campus.

Before one can talk about the beginning of something, one must go backward to find the origins of the story. From as far back as the 1980s, the East Stroudsburg Area School District's enrollment was growing. Relocatable classrooms were brought into the various campuses, intended to provide temporary relief, but were becoming the norm.

The brunt of this growth was likely felt the most by Middle Smithfield Elementary School, located on Route 209. In the early 1990s, it was the northernmost school in the district. Though it underwent a major renovation with the addition of eight classrooms, a new cafeteria and library in 1982, it was already overcrowded within the following ten years. "We were getting so big, we had to add pods to the school," says John Doyle, a custodian at Middle Smithfield. "It was kinda deceiving because people that would look at the front of the school wouldn't realize how many pods we had. They were all back behind the school."

Middle Smithfield Elementary School

Construction of a new elementary school on Route 402 soon began to help relieve the overcrowding at Middle Smithfield. The "Route 402 School," as it was referred to in the planning stages, was officially named "Resica Elementary School" for its township in January 1994. Gregory Naudascher, who had been serving as the principal of Middle Smithfield, was selected to open Resica the next fall. By its fourth year, Resica, too, was overcrowded, and a "pod" building was added to the campus to house its fifth-grade classes.

While the elementary school classrooms filled, similar overcrowding happened at J.T. Lambert Intermediate School. Patricia Mulroy, a health and physical education teacher there, recalls the overcrowding conditions. "We didn't have enough classrooms. Sometimes our health classes were in the teachers' classrooms, or we taught in the auditorium. At one point, there was about 1900 kids." To address these changes, the district added a "pod" building behind the school and lockers in the auditorium. "Our population was booming," said Kevin Nace. "The entire time I was [at the South High School], we were building schools."

Resica Elementary School was not the only new school in the plans. As far back as November 1993, discussions took place at board meetings for land investigation in the Bushkill area. Additional elementary schools were taking shape, but the students in these elementary schools needed a place to matriculate. At the January 23, 1995 meeting of the board, the superintendent, Dr. John Grogan, "stated there were no plans for a new high school." The administration acknowledged that "there is an immediate need for construction and renovation at the high school. At the same time, there is a need to pursue the purchase of land and new construction." A parent in the district and member of the school board, Steve Lastra, brought to everyone's attention that 51% of the students in the district live above Marshalls Creek. It was now becoming increasingly clear that there was a need to build more than just an elementary school in Bushkill.

Less than a month later, on February 13, 1995, a prominent statement was printed in the board meeting minutes:

The 400+ acres that the district is presently looking at in the Bushkill area will comfortably hold two Resica Schools, a school the size of JTL and also one the size of the high school presently occupied… including grounds, playing fields and parking areas. MOTION CARRIED.

This project was soon named "the North Site" and became a popular topic of conversation at board meetings. By February of 1996, it was reported that the Lehman County Planning Commission, was "very receptive to our plans for the North Site Schools." Lawrence Marcial, who was hired in 1994 as a high school social studies teacher, recalls the rationale for this growth:

There was a massive migration from particularly New York City out into the Poconos. Monroe County was getting the brunt of that. And since East Stroudsburg School District covers a bit of southern Pike county and a bit of Monroe County, there was discussion on how best to reorganize the school to adapt to this. The population growth was in those gated communities and lake-based private communities in Pike County, and that's where they decided to build the school to adjust to the population growth and put a school where many of the new families were moving.

Proponents developed plans for a new high school and intermediate school for the North Site along Bushkill Falls Road in Pike County. For reasons unknown, the district decided to construct one building that housed both an intermediate school and a high school. Other than the auditorium, natatorium, nurse's office, and cafeteria, the two schools would operate completely separately.

One pressing question was what to name the North Site elementary School, which was to share the design of Resica. Eventually, it was decided that the elementary school would be named Bushkill Elementary School. Eric Forsyth, who is the District's Director of Communications and Operations, recalls this massive project. "The first building up there was the sewer treatment plant along with the water tower services building. That became the hub. It was our first experience as a district with an installation of that size." Construction of Bushkill Elementary School began in July, 1997.

During the 1997-98 school year, Middle Smithfield Elementary was a major hub of excited energy. Aside from the daily activities involved with educating children, the principal, Eva Haddon, had been selected to open Bushkill Elementary School. The new school boasted over fifty-five classrooms for a student population of about 1,000 students.

In 1998, Haddon and both office secretaries, the guidance counselor, two cafeteria aides, and twenty teachers moved from Middle Smithfield up to the new school in Lehman Township. Teachers like Kristen Bueki, Deborah Sands, Elyse Vitchers, and Linda Wisneiski were among the first to teach at Bushkill and became long-time members of the new community.

The opening of Bushkill Elementary School was a new beginning for the East Stroudsburg Area School District. It was the first school built on the North Site, a considerably different environment than the other schools in the district.

Bushkill Elementary School

Teachers immediately realized just how secluded the new campus was. "I remember driving up there one day and there was a huge coyote sitting next to the sign!" recalls Sandra Borrasso, who was a special education teacher in the district. "We would get announcements, 'there is no outside recess today because mama bear and her cubs are on the playground!' which happened quite often!"

As the first school year continued, concerns about weather began to circulate among the faculty. Nadia Worobij, who taught music at Bushkill when the school opened, clearly remembers the winter of 1998–99 at Bushkill.

> We were the only school that was up there. The first couple of winters, until the middle school and high school were built, were treacherous because the roads were not maintained. I remember a lot of the teachers were fearful that we might have to stay over night, so we always had extra food and clothes ready, just in case. A lot of teachers were terrified that first year, but after that, they got much better at maintaining the roads.

As the community became increasingly aware of the new intermediate and high schools under construction, the North Site became a popular topic of discussion at Board meetings. In particular, parents and students alike wanted to know who would be required to attend the new school. "It seems like every board meeting, they would divide the district with a line in a different place," said Jim Reynolds. "The board changed their minds a number of times on where the line was. Who was going to the North and who was going to the South."

East Stroudsburg High School, which soon became known as the "South High School," had become extremely overcrowded. Carty, who was serving as assistant principal, recalls his last two years in this building.

> When we were in the original East Stroudsburg High School, our numbers rose to somewhere in the neighborhood of seventeen to eighteen hundred students, and the capacity for that building was about eight hundred. So, we were using the [Bunnell build ing], and I believe we had something in the neighborhood of seventeen to nineteen modular classrooms down behind the building. So, there was a definite need to split into two high schools.

Between 1996 and 2000, many new teachers were hired in anticipation of the eventual opening of the North Site. Many of these teachers ended up occupying modular classrooms, which were situated behind the main high school building and connected by wooden ramps.

Sean Edwards teaching in a modular classroom at the soon-to-be South High School, spring 2000

"If you walked out the back doors, there were modular trailers along the football field," said Sean Edwards, who was hired in 1999. "So, the entire social studies department plus half of the special education department was in trailers. The senior class was over four-hundred kids." Karen Mochan, née Haas, remembers her first year, "I roamed between trailers outside, and then my second year there, I had my own trailer. It was a different experience because in order to go up and get your mail, photocopy, go to the faculty room, you were going outside and walking up the back stairwell in the rain and the snow and everything. It was an experience!" Naturally, such a crowded building can be intimidating for a new teacher. Julie Tischler, née Frank, was hired mid-year in 1999 as an art teacher and recalls some consolation from a colleague. "I remember Billy David was down there. I remember him stopping me in the hallway and saying, 'please don't think it's like this all the time. Please don't base the experience on this year. This is a terrible year.'"

The students felt similarly to the faculty, as 2001 graduate Randy Paolino recalls. "I remember feeling like the school was massively packed, the hallways were always jam-packed between classes." The prospect of opening a new school began to appeal to everybody as it would provide much-needed relief on the existing buildings.

The decision to open a new high school and intermediate school had been made, construction had begun, and staff had been hired to staff the schools. The next decision that needed to be made was a critical one: Who would be the principal?

In 1999, Michael Michaels accepted the role of Director of Human Resources, and Carty's fellow assistant principal, Irene Duggins, was selected to replace Michaels as the principal of the existing High School. Now, the district had a second high school principal position to fill, and Carty decided that he wanted to apply for the position. "Given the background of working in the South, I had aspirations of becoming the principal."

Carty knew that this would not be a simple process, and he wanted to be prepared. So, he reached out to Angelo Senese, who was an administrator in the Pleasant Valley School District, and a personal friend.

Senese, like Carty, enjoyed playing golf. Wanting an opportunity to ask questions and gain some advice, Carty invited Senese out to play golf at the Shawnee Inn. With a pad and pen in hand, Carty was prepared to ask lots of questions. To Carty's surprise, Senese did not answer his questions. Rather, Senese told him the questions he would need to be able to answer. "Angelo said to me, 'Now, you're going to need to know something about this, and make sure that you know this, and make sure you know that…'"

Upon finishing the twenty-seventh hole on the course, Carty was shaking his head. Angelo noticed this and said, "it's a lot of information, isn't it? Well, now you've got a lot of homework to do." "I was thinking that he was gonna give me all the answers," said Carty. "He didn't give me answers, all he did was give me questions. And then, I had to research all of this." Looking back, Carty was really appreciative of Senese's approach to mentoring. "I learned from that, because if he had given me the answers, would I have prepared as hard as I did? No, I wouldn't." As the interview date approached, Carty heeded Senese's suggestions and read about every topic that might be asked about by the hiring committee.

On a warm summer day in 1999, Carty walked into the board room for his interview. Sitting in the room was a panel of ten people, including a district principal, several teachers, the superintendent, and a member of the school board. "I walked in and they were all sitting in a semi-circle, while I was given a little chair in the middle of the room." Feeling the tension of the situation, Carty tried to lighten the mood. Across the room sat a pitcher of water and a glass. "I walked over and said, 'You don't mind if I pour myself a glass of water before I go before the firing squad, do you?' I tried to lighten the mood by pouring the glass of water. A few people laughed."

Despite the severity of the interview, Carty was not nervous, as he knew that he was prepared. The committee must have liked what they heard, and on August 19, 1999, Carty was appointed principal of the East Stroudsburg North High School.

Minutes of the September 27, 1999 school board meeting, approving Carty's appointment as principal of the North High School.

Around the same time that Carty underwent the interview process, the district made similar hires for the neighboring Lehman Intermediate School. Rosa Calvet, a graduate of Barry College and long-time English teacher, and Donna Albright, who had a background in teaching health and physical education, were hired to plan and open the new intermediate school that would share a building with the North High School. Unlike the high school side, the intermediate school was structured to have classrooms, computer labs, and science labs on each floor. Further, the tiles, carpeting, and bulletin boards were color-coded by floor, inspiring Calvet to designate "houses" with members of grades six, seven, and eight belonging to either the green, red, or blue house.

Carty and Calvet had their work cut out for them. "Once I was hired as the principal," said Carty, "it was my job to basically order everything that went into that school. Anything that wasn't placed by a contractor, I was responsible for. Student desks, teacher desks, office furniture, filing cabinets, all the custodial equipment, computers… shelving…it kept me pretty busy!"

Carla Mathiesen, who taught German in the high school, remembers Carty welcoming everyone's input during this process. "Our last year [at South], he was constantly calling people into his office and saying, 'So let me show you…what do you think about this desk? Let me show you this catalog. What do you think of these chairs? Do you think these would look good in the classrooms?'" "That was pretty neat," said Debra Padavano. "He had a lot to buy. You don't realize what goes into a building!"

Few people understand the challenge of purchasing everything that is needed to open a school, particularly regarding the items that most people do not notice. Custodial equipment and supplies typically fall into this category. So, Carty sought the advice of Kieran Pryor, who was the head custodian at the South campus.

Kieran Pryor, 1996

"Kieran went through a lot of the needs and wants of what they were going to put in as far as ordering," said fellow custodian Tim Harris. Pryor helped Carty find the answers to questions most people seldom consider, such as how much toilet paper must one buy for a new building, how many mops should be purchased, and a myriad of other small but crucial details. "District operations involve a lot of areas that most people never see," added Forsyth. "Services get delivered from locations they would never imagine, there is equipment in places people wouldn't suspect."

Another responsibility Carty had was staffing the building. "There were staff members who did not want to go North, and there was talk that if people didn't volunteer, they would be involuntarily transferred based on their number of years of service," said Carty. Fortunately, Carty's hiring was received very positively by the faculty. "I hope that my hiring had some to do with people volunteering," said Carty. "At first, nobody wanted to go to the North school from the South," said Robert Green. "It wasn't until they chose Mr. Carty that a lot of people from the South came to the North. He had a big following and people went with him because he has such a good disposition and such a good outlook on everything." "He's the reason I decided to move North," said Bill David. "At the time, I was the Dean of Students when the split happened, and Carty was a close professional colleague of mine. He was the assistant principal and I was the dean of students that worked with him closely. So, when he was placed at the North High School, I went along with him."

In some instances, Carty personally invited staff members to come to the North High School.

One in particular was Susan Wilson, who was the librarian at Resica Elementary School. "I was surprised when Rico brought it up to me how exciting it was to have this challenge of working with this grade level, which I had never worked with before, nine to twelve. No other librarian in the district wanted to do it, and I told Rico 'Yes' and it was a wonderful decision for me." He also encouraged custodians to join the staff at the North campus, as recalled by John Doyle. "In 1999, going into 2000, Mr. Carty asked me to be his day custodian up there. I had a nice rapport with him, and I decided it would be a good time to try something different in my life."

Another important hiring decision needed to be made, and that was who would serve as the custodial supervisor for the North Campus would be. Tim Harris, who had served as a custodian at the South High School since 1988, remembers Carty approaching him with an opportunity. "[Carty and I] talked about them needing a head custodian for up North. I really wasn't sure if I wanted to do it or not, and Mr. Carty gave the old 'why not you, why shouldn't you do it.'" Eventually, Harris agreed to interview for the position and was selected to serve as the custodial supervisor for the North Campus.

Ultimately, the original staff of the North High School included both new and experienced teachers, some of whom came from the South High School, while others came from J.T. Lambert and the elementary schools. In addition to hiring teachers and support staff, an assistant principal needed to be hired. The district found their candidate in January 2000, when James McGovern was interviewed. "He came from Crestwood High School in between Hazleton and Wilkes-Barre," said Carty. "I'd say that I had some input but not one-hundred percent in choosing my assistant, but was very pleased with the choice." McGovern, who had previously taught English, had recently completed his administrative certification. "To this day, I still think [Carty] is the best mentor I ever had," said McGovern.

James McGovern, the first assistant principal at North

"We were able to communicate well. Completely honest with one another. So, it was just a real good fit, a good mesh of personalities and philosophy." David remembers McGovern as "a really good guy and really got kids. He wanted to be involved. He was the same mold as Mr. Carty. He gets kids, meet kids where they're at, support them as much as you possibly can to make them successful."

One of Carty and McGovern's first tasks was to hire new faculty and staff. Given the location of the school, Carty offered a suggestion to the director of personnel."Let's focus our recruiting in the Scranton area. There's a lot of people out there looking for jobs and they could be at the North site in forty-five minutes to an hour. So, we recruited a lot people from that area." To this day, several of North's faculty members commute from the Scranton vicinity.

Purchasing and hiring are vital tasks for the establishment of a new school, but Carty also realized that there were equally important matters, though less tangible, that needed his attention. Aside from the similarities that the North and South High Schools would have, one thing that South had was a community. "They were trying to build a community around a school," said business teacher Jason Kish. "And the way the communities were up there, there were so many pockets." Carty's vision was to build a community around that school, and he knew that in order to do that, he had to get to know the students who would be attending there. McGovern recalls this endeavor:

> Mr. Carty had done a great deal of work establishing relationships with students that he knew would be attending the school, and had them become leaders. And that process all started prior to the school opening. He had done such a remarkable job.

Indeed, students were valuable members of the planning process. "Many people believe that 'a child should be seen, not heard.' I believe they need to be heard, and you need to listen to what they're saying!" said Carty. "They want to know that you're listening. The students need to be a part of planning that school. I couldn't have done it without them."

For many students, interactions with the principal only take place when rules have been violated. Carty took it upon himself to interact with many of the students who would be attending the North High School, even before the building opened. Paolino remembers his first interaction with Carty:

I remember meeting him, I believe, my sophomore year during baseball tryouts. He was a baseball guy and while we were at try-outs, he showed up. At the beginning of try-outs, usually the first thing you do is start throwing the ball around to loosen up, and I don't remember having a partner and must have been just standing there. Mr. Carty came up to me and said 'hey, do you want to throw?' 'Yeah, sure.' I remember as a young kid, thinking, 'oh wow, one of the teachers is asking to throw with me,' and that was the first time I met him.

Carty also strove to establish a good rapport with the parents of North students. "He was able to get along with the parents and understand them and help them solve problems," said Reynolds. "A lot of people have trouble with that. He also had the support of a lot of parents up there. That was important."

Unfortunately, not everyone felt positively about the new school. There was a lot of negative perception throughout the community. "There was a lot of fighting over the lines, where the lines would be drawn," recalls Carty. "And some people did not want their children to go to the North High School. Some felt they lived closer to the existing school. It would be an inconvenience for them to come up there for different events. So, there was a lot of negativity about the whole 'splitting the school' and their children going there."

Carty, being the principal, did his best to help people see the good in going to the North High School. "That created the biggest challenge, because it was our job to dismiss the 'this is a bad place' or the negatives." At numerous board meetings, Carty would stay after and talk with parents. "They would say, 'I don't want my kids going there!' and I would tell them, 'it'll be all right, we'll get this done.'"

Additionally, the class of 2001, who were to be the first senior class in the new school, was given the choice of which high school they would attend for their senior year. "The first year, the seniors were given a choice," said Carty. "They had the choice of staying at the original East Stroudsburg or what now is known as South High School. And if they chose to [stay at South], they had to provide their own transportation. There wouldn't be any bussing for them." Only seventy-five seniors elected to attend East Stroudsburg North.

Carty believed that opening a new school meant creating a new culture, and this became the rationale for how many decisions were made. "The biggest challenge was creating a new culture and getting everyone to buy in that this was gonna be a good school and they would be afforded the same opportunities they would have in the original high school," said Carty. Kevin Nace fondly recalls this process:

North was just a chance to break off and do something different: be whatever we envisioned it to be as the people who came in first, and a lot of that vision came from the kids. And I thought that Mr. Carty is really good at certain things, and one thing he's really good at is listening to the needs and the wants of the kids. What do you want this building to be? How do you want it to be?

When one considers the culture and identify of a school, what quickly comes to mind are the school's mascot, colors, and logo. "To a lot of outside people, they would say that's not important. But that's the basis of your culture and how you build your school pride," said David. At the November 16, 1998 school board meeting, the school colors for the North campus were decided upon: purple and white. This was not well received by students or faculty. "We didn't know at first," said Mathiesen, "when they were originally planning, they thought [the colors] would have something to do with purple. Then, the first incoming senior class for North, when they realized that the decision was being made for them...they made their concerns known. And the next thing you know, they're storming the school board meeting, saying 'we don't want those colors.'"

EAST STROUDSBURG
HIGH SCHOOLS
NORTH/SOUTH CAMPUS

PROGRAM OF STUDIES

2000 — 2001

GRADES 9, 10, 11 and 12

The 2000–2001 Program of Studies, designed using what was intended to be the colors and logo for both the North and South High Schools

Charles Dailey, who was a physical education teacher at J.T. Lambert and was to move to the North High School, agreed with the students' thinking. "It was a foregone conclusion that we were going to be 'the musketeers.' I, for one, was having none of that!" While the students were advocating for their own colors and mascot choice, the faculty made their voices known, too. Dailey said, at the time, "we need to let the kids have a little input in how this goes down."

Carty, too, believed that the students should have a say in the matter, and encouraged students to develop a petition. "There was a group of students who then held a contest to decide what the mascot's name would be, and also the school colors. That was all student-generated," said Carty. In November 1999, the school colors once again became a topic of discussion at the board meeting, and the students at the South High School were officially given permission to conduct a survey. The students devised a list of choices that were printed onto a ballot sheet. "We were then given the opportunity to choose between purple and silver, and the musketeers; or green and white; or our current colors, or we could've also chosen the Trailblazers or the Knights," said Dailey.

One month later, district superintendent John Grogan asked Carty to share the findings of the survey for the board. Of the 1200 students who received the survey, 900 responded, and the majority's decision was for the mascot to be the Timberwolf. The school colors would be Carolina blue, black, and silver. The back story of this effort was later published in the front of North's first yearbook:

People have wondered why the school mascot of East Stroudsburg Area High School-North is the Timberwolf. Timberwolves are worthy, noble, honorable, and mighty animals. The display extreme power and intense sense of leadership. Timberwolves can be intimidating alone, but together, as a pack they dominate. Timberwolves do not have many predators, which makes them a respected animal. The students responsible for choosing the mascot had certain criteria to follow before a proper mascot could be named.

Last year, a group of sophomores who would be attending the

North site in the fall started a petition. The petition stated that they believed that the students should have some choice in deciding the school mascot and colors. The students attended board meetings that opposed the idea of Musketeers with the colors of purple and white. Permission was granted to send out ballots to all students going north. Then the students with the help of teachers searched for a mascot.

The Timberwolf looked the strongest and the colors of Carolina Blue, Black, and Silver seemed to be the perfect choice. The school colors were originally going to be purple and white, but the students felt that since the schools would be separate then they should have a different identity. The mascot was finally named the Timberwolves due to the determination and forethought of the North student body. THE STRENGTH IS IN THE PACK.

School pride was already developing, and the doors had not even opened yet. Students were proud of the culture they were helping to build, and though the community had not yet fully embraced the new school, the overall attitude about it was improving. While the school identity needed to be developed, so did the educational mission of the school. As the principal, Carty was tasked with writing the school's mission statement, which remains the same today:

Our mission is to educate the students of East Stroudsburg Area Senior High School-North by providing a diversity of experiences in a challenging academic environment so that our students aspire to high academic achievement and develop character, community spirit, intellectual curiosity, and a lifelong dedication to learning.

Generally speaking, a mission statement does not stand out in a student's mind. The logo of the school, on the other hand, is often remembered years after one graduates. "We felt," said Carty, "that if we were going to create a new identity and a new culture that we needed our own identity." Two faculty members contributed to the original branding of the school, one being Craig Long, who taught technology education at the South High School.

Starting a new school, they needed an identity. Once [Carty] got some teachers on board…he brought us all together and said, 'we're gonna create an identity. We have to call ourselves something, pick our colors… et cetera.' There were a few teachers that he trusted—I was one of them, and I feel proud of that. I designed the logo from a graphic arts point of view.

Another teacher, MaryGrace Anderson, contributed to the branding by drawing the "wolf head" logo that was used on stationery and school publications over the first six years at North. "Overwhelmingly, the kids liked the Timberwolf idea," she remembers. Anderson also designed the academic shield that appeared on report cards and diplomas for several years. Thankfully, the district administration approved of the new identity.

"I was fine with that," said Douglas Arnold, who, by 1999, was serving as the Assistant Superintendent for Pupil Services. "They weren't going to be the Cavaliers and if they needed their own identity, why not let them have that. Even if you had the same colors, how would that solve any issues? I don't think we would've enjoyed great price savings by buying identical uniforms. It did give them a feel for who they were to become."

With much of the front-facing aspects of the school in place, Carty still had his work cut out for him. In reading the educational philosophy of the new school, one could see Carty's goals very clearly articulated.

The primary purpose of the educational community at East Stroudsburg Area Senior High School-North is to prepare thinking and responsible citizens for life in an ever-changing and complex society. To insure success, students, parents, teachers, administrators and support staff should take an active role in the total school program, while encouraging and nurturing academic and social development.

Indeed, the success of the school would not be possible without the input of students and their families, as well as the entire staff. Fortunately, this was achieved rather quickly and the planning of this new school was a highly collaborative venture. Additionally,

In an increasingly pluralistic society, we endeavor to teach students to strive for justice and fairness and to eliminate discrimination and intolerance. Diversity must be accommodated within unity, the two being complementary rather than in opposition.

It was clear from the outset that the student body would be a diverse one, from the standpoint of cultural ethnicity and socioeconomic background. The celebration of these differences was established early on and a no tolerance policy toward bullying was immediately enforced. Moreover,

In an effort to help students achieve these goals, high school teachers and administrators participate in professional development seminars focusing on continuous examination of instructional methods and modifications of practice. As a staff, we believe that student-centered classrooms will be critical in helping develop social, emotion, physical and academic skills.

The above philosophy informed how Carty mentored his staff but also how students were treated.

"Mr. Carty seemed to me less concerned about what was going on at the state level," recalled Mathiesen. "'Don't worry about that, let's worry about what is going on in our building. Let's make sure we are doing the best we can for this community and these kids.'"

In addition to hiring teachers, departmental leadership needed to be established. Veteran department chairs Robert Green (technology education) and Bill David (science) continued to serve in their roles at the North High School. "I was excited about the opportunity to become part of the new building and have a chance to help build a new culture," said David. "I believed in what Mr. Carty believed in, and I wanted to go along with him." In quick succession, Kevin Nace was selected to be the Social Studies Department Chair, Eric Anderson as the English Department Chair, and Karen Haas as the Chair of the Math Department.

A school principal is generally permitted a good amount of autonomy in decision-making. However, many decisions are made above their heads, particularly regarding the physical plant. The building, which was designed by The Architectural Studio, Allentown, and constructed by the Skepton Construction Company, based in Pennsburg, allotted 240,630 square feet to the high school side of the building.

The school's general layout encompassed three wings that were connected by a main hallway. While Carty had no input in the design of the building, he was tasked with determining space utilization, furnishing it, and purchasing equipment.

"There were certain wings designed for music, there were certain wings designed for tech ed, and the science labs were all together," said Carty. "There was basically just one wing that was three floors. I had to decide where we were going to put social studies, math, and English." "When Mr. Carty took over," recalled Nace, "he decided we were going to put our hallways in as departments. There's an English hallway, a math hallway, and a social studies hallway. I chose where social studies was going to be. That the input I had, and that was the only input I had." Mathiesen remembers the optimism involved in planning a new school, even down to determining locations for classes. "It was fun just to go in his office and just dreaming.

The first floor of the classroom wing, which houses the Social Studies Department.

It was all dreams and hopes and trying to plan out how they all worked together." "Special ed was divided throughout the building; we weren't in the basement anymore," said Padavano. "I was a para in the emotional support room [at South], and it was in the basement of the building. It was much more segregated by class. Up at North, it was more a community, I felt, with the teachers. I taught emotional support but [my classroom] was up in the math wing."

The three hallways that branched off of the main hallway were sometimes referred to as "fingers." Carty remembers inviting long-time social studies teacher, Clark Stem, to transfer to North High School. "I asked him to pick which classroom he wanted. I asked him, 'do you want a view of the woods, or a view of the middle finger?' He laughed and said, 'I'll take a view of the woods.'" Room 127 became Stem's classroom, which, as promised, offered a lovely view of the Delaware State Forest. The three-floor classroom wing, or "Wing L," as it is labeled on the building map, housed social studies on the first floor, math on the second floor, and English on the third floor. Health classes utilized two classrooms in the social studies wing, French and German classes were held on the second floor, Spanish classes were on the third floor, and special education classrooms were on all three floors. Much of this configuration remained the same for the first decade, and as of this writing, the three academic departments are still situated on these floors.

Once spaces were assigned, materials and equipment needed to be purchased. Together, Carty and McGovern worked long hours to ensure that this new school would have what was needed to operate. "My decisions more were curricular, perhaps some textbooks, establishing caps on the numbers of students in classes," McGovern remembers. "We were spending half the day at the South campus and then doing walk-throughs in the North campus."

Technology was a major concern in this new building, ensuring that each classroom was properly outfitted, and all equipment was functional. Bob Green recalls several trips to the campus during construction to determine what needed to be done. "It took a lot of time to set these facilities up. A lot of people put in a lot of hours on their own to get things set up. You don't realize how much is involved with equipping a building. You overlook things. Overhead projectors in every room, where does the electric have to be...the computer rooms all needed networks."

Establishing a technological infrastructure in a new facility is a frustrating process, however, it was also appealing for teachers. "One of the reasons I wanted to go up there was because the South High School equipment was very antiquated," said Long. "I was teaching SuperPaint on old Macs down there. I could only go so far with that. So, one of the enticements about going up there was getting all new computers, all new equipment, all this new software." The business department shared a similar enthusiasm for the new facilities they would be teaching in at the new school. Jason Kish was fortunate enough to have both a classroom and a computer laboratory for his General Business courses.

I had a classroom with desks — that's where we would do book work — and in the course at the time, half of the class was learning the skill of keyboarding or typing. I would teach the business aspect and then transfer into the computer lab, which, at the time, was state-of-the-art. Brand new computers. At the original campus when I taught at East Stroudsburg that first year, [I was] teaching keyboarding on actual typewriters. So, when we converted to the North campus, we were now using computers, and that was amazing to teach on the newer technology.

As construction moved steadily along, the athletic program was already well underway. Dailey, who was hired as the high school's head football coach, had his work cut out for him during the summer of 2000. "None of our locker room facilities or our practice fields were ready to go that first day, so we initially housed our equipment in the Bushkill Elementary gym, and we practiced on the Lehman practice field." As the building became safe for occupancy, Dailey and his coaching staff put in long hours to prepare for the opening of the school. "I remember being there through the night getting our weight room set up," said Dailey. "We were all excited," recalls Bruce Berke, who coached football under Dailey. "You're opening a new school, so it's like Christmas. Everything is brand new. As a football coach, I was able to go up there before the normal student population. We were able to see the grounds. It was a brand-new football program; we were excited about that."

Timberwolves Football Coaching Staff, Fall 2000

In the Fall 2000 Game Day Program, Dailey penned a message that speaks not only to football, but entering new frontiers.

> When I step back and take in the magnitude of what we (the East Stroudsburg North family) are about to embark upon I am awe struck. This is history. With every decision made, every action taken, we are moving into uncharted territory. We need to embrace this challenge and lay the foundation for generations to come. Each and every one of us will claim our own little piece of history and together we can blaze a trail of pride, respect, discipline and loyalty from which our traditions will grow. Thank you for coming out and giving your support to our young people. It is greatly appreciated. On behalf of the entire Timberwolves' football program, I thank you.

Often a high school football program requires the support of a booster club. One parent, Diane Krupski, realized this and approached Dailey to inquire. "I asked him who was going to take over the booster club," she remembers. "He said to me, 'wait right here,' and he came back with an envelope with a bunch of papers, handed it to me, and he said, 'you are!' I became the booster mom for all the sports when the school opened."

Two years prior to North opening, Carty's long-time friend Mark Brown replaced Jim Reynolds as the District's Athletic Director. When the North campus was underway, it was decided to hire an Associate Athletic Director for each high school. Selected for this role at North was Bill David. "Billy is a great guy," recalls Brown. "When North opened, he transferred up to North. An absolutely outstanding person for that time. He taught part of the day and was the athletic director at North. He was great not just in the planning stages but in the multitude of decisions when you hit the ground running with a new athletic program."

Even prior to opening the doors, the North had established itself from the South campus in name, mascot, and colors, but these were not the only differences. Since North High School had a much smaller student population, due to so few seniors choosing to attend

North, competing with larger, more established schools would not be easy. So, Brown decided to put the North school in the Lackawanna League, housed in the Pennsylvania Interscholastic Athletic Association's District 11. "I really think it made much more sense having them twenty-five minutes from Wallenpaupack, thirty minutes from Delaware Valley, twenty-five minutes from North Pocono, and half an hour from Western Wayne," said Brown. "We were so much smaller than the other schools that were in the league that the South played in," said David. "So, we did a lot of traveling not to where kids would have traditionally been used to playing in the Lehigh Valley area, or Palmerton, or Lehighton, or those schools." "We were traveling to some very far venues to play because the Lackawanna conference is huge. We were going up to Montrose and places we'd never heard of," Dailey remembers. "The coaching staff at North appreciated the support [Carty] gave them, because they were young teachers and coaches and he was very supportive of them," said Frank Johnson.

Carty wanted everybody in the building to feel important. Such a simple yet important desire formed the foundation on which Carty led the school.

> Everybody was important to me. Whether you are a custodian, or a secretary, or a teacher, or an instructional aide, or a student... we all had a job to do. Granted, my job was different than theirs. But I looked at it as my job was no more important than theirs. And if everybody's doing their job, you've got a well-run team. And that's pretty much the way I operated.

This belief presented itself not only through his interactions with students and staff, but in decision-making. Having worked at an established high school for nearly twenty years, Carty observed how things were done and, while some things he agreed with, other practices he did not. "When we were at South, we had assigned staff parking, and depending on your seniority, you parked closer to the building," said Carty. This led to constant arguments due to people comparing their years of service with other employees, and the anger that erupted when a substitute teacher would innocently park in someone's space. "When I became principal up at North, one of the first questions a teacher asked me at a staff meeting was, 'Will there be assigned parking?' I said, 'absolutely not.'" Carty pointed at one of the lots on the campus map and said, "That lot will be considered staff parking. That probably will not hold everyone on the staff. The upper lot, which is up behind Lehman, is the overflow. It's a little further away from the building. If you don't like your spot, get here earlier. No one will have an assigned parking spot, including me." Naturally, people are creatures of habit, and many tended to park in the same area, but under Carty's tenure, no parking spots were assigned to any employee.

Construction took shape at the North campus, and soon it would be time to start loading in furniture, equipment, and school supplies. One afternoon, the custodial staff gathered on the then-unfinished campus. John Doyle took his first look at the building and thought, "What did I get myself into?" The head custodian, Tim Harris, asked the staff if they had any concerns. "I told them, 'Getting up those mountains in the wintertime," said Doyle. "There are no shoulders, and it is like night-and-day between up here and down there!"

It was not long before the staff grew accustomed to the new, scenic commute they had. Not only were staff members arriving, but equipment and materials were on their way. Loading in the many, many boxes soon began. "The first forty days we were able to get in there to start to move things in," said Harris. "We worked every day for forty days, including Saturdays and Sundays." "We used the cafeteria of Lehman and North… as the staging area for a lot of stuff because the cafeteria was the only place with a loading dock," Doyle recalls. "The elevators weren't even working yet. I was carrying two overhead carts at a time up three flights of stairs." During much of the freight delivery, Doyle operated a forklift to move palates into the building. One delivery in particular will stay with Doyle forever.

I got the luck of the draw to unload the wood lathe, which was very, very heavy. The company packed it on this thin pine skid. I got that off the truck and my plan was to lower it, but then the whole palate exploded, and the wood lathe hit the ground and gets destroyed. Ruined beyond repair, and it was a lot of money. So, the joke was, 'we got everything in the building except for that really expensive piece, Johnny!' It was a complete accident.

Due to the number of materials arriving each day, the central receiving area, located below the gymnasium, quickly filled up. So, staging areas were set up in the intermediate school library, the high school gym, and in various other classrooms on the first floor.

By mid-August, teachers were permitted to enter the building and set up their classrooms. Aside from the new facility, its location was also new to many of the teachers who had never ventured up to Lehman Township before. "I remember the first time I drove up to see the school and thinking 'Wow, it's really one mile south of Canada!'" said Mathiesen. Ryan Frable, who would be teaching math in the North High School, remembers thinking "This is in the middle of nowhere. This is in the middle of the Delaware State Forest, and all the sudden, this monstrosity of a complex just appears!" Another math teacher, Edward Zasada, remembers, "The first time I ever tried to find the place, I got lost." "I went to the campus, and it was still just dirt, cinder blocks, and cars," remembered Kevin Voglino, who taught in the English Department. "And I remember meeting Mr. Carty there actually. He was there in the parking lot and he talked to me for an hour or so, and he showed me around the school! He was so helpful and very friendly, and that was a great start."

Once most of the structural work was complete, many were impressed by the appearance of the building. "It was huge, it was like a community college," said Tischler. "I thought it was beautiful, and it was not done, and we opened the first year with it not really being done." "I thought it was rather industrial to look at," said Arnold, "but on the other hand, it was innovative in some of the ways they were doing things."

If you ask anybody who worked in the North High School during its first year, they will likely share vivid memories of navigating the new space prior to the school year beginning. Supplies were still arriving each day, as teacher Sean Edwards recalls. "You walked in the front door, there were boxes of desks, TVs, books, down the entire hallway as far as you can see." Construction was still underway and would continue well into the first year of the school. "I remember no ceiling tiles where you could see wires hanging," said Lori Soskil, who was a newly-hired science teacher. "I remember ceramic tiles needing to be completed. Boxes…and boxes!" Soskil recalls having to make many trips over to Lehman's library to pick up all of the science lab materials and transport them over to the high school science wing.

As to be expected in any construction project, there were setbacks, confusion, and the occasional error. Karen Mochan remembers receiving her classroom assignment, and to her surprise, such a room did not exist. "I was supposed to be in room 233, which does not exist. 231 is the last room in our wing, which is my classroom now. I remember being in the hallways and panicking, '233? That would be the boy's bathroom!' And when they figured out it was 231, I walked in and I had three teachers' worth of belongings in my room because they didn't know where to put anything!"

Though the faculty members had their work cut out for them in setting up their classrooms, the impression seems to be that they were pleased with the building's appearance. "I'll never forget walking up there for the first time and seeing the library," said Wilson. "It was so beyond anything I had ever worked in because it had a funkiness to it with the exposed beams and the crazy windows from floor to ceiling which I absolutely loved!" It was not long before the faculty realized how well-equipped this new facility was technologically. Kevin Nace fondly remembers his first impressions of the North High School.

I taught [at South] and when I came up here, everything was so clean and new, and it was exciting. I walked into my class room… and [Carty] says, 'This is gonna be your room!' Brand new desks, brand new chairs, everything matches, everything looks right. There's a TV hanging on the wall, and I thought, 'Oh my God, I get my own TV? We don't have a cart that we have to track around every room and put in two weeks ahead of time that I need a cart from the A/V guy?' Everything about it was new and different and really exciting, but more than that, everything was just clean and fresh. It was the technology that everybody wanted.

For some departments where specialized equipment and facilities were needed, additional setbacks came up. "I vaguely remember there was a hiccup with the ordering before we moved into the school," recalls MaryGrace Anderson. "There was a big cancelation of furniture so I remember we re-ordered from a different company. I would teach with whatever arrived in the classroom. I think the art tables finally came in March. It was fun. You just made do." Bradley Pawlikowski, who was hired that summer as the school's instrumental music teacher, remembers other challenges associated with a band program following the splitting of a high school.

> When we divided from one school to another, there was no thought process of 'two French horns go here; two French horns go there.' It's simply geographic, so you were dealt with the hand of cards that you had.

The shop rooms presented their own unique challenges, such as equipment set up, electric lines, dust collectors, among other things. "I was up there a few times looking to see if it was ready," said Green. "And it really wasn't but we had to open. Trying to make sure they did certain things in the shop rooms."

The clock was ticking. August was quickly passing by, and both the construction crews and the faculty worked frantically to prepare for the first day of school. "I still remember there was a week to go, and it look there was two months to go!" McGovern remembers. "The delivery of certain things, phones in the room, making sure the desks were all set up. It took a lot. I remember the week before school we were still wearing hard hats in the halls." Carty recalls this period as chaotic. "I didn't want to open, we weren't ready, but we didn't have a choice. It was a mess, very chaotic."

Though the time constraint was stressful, what was already successful was collaboration among the staff. "There was a lot of cooperation between the custodial staff between the South and the North. Mr. Carty made that happen. He got people on the same page and working together," said Green. "Rico had to take care of the project and the planning and setting up the school," said Kish. "The actual work that he had to do in planning all of that…it must've been an amazing workload! But they did it!"

The main entrance, natatorium, and gynmasium entrance as they looked in 2000

A front-page story in *The Pocono Record* offered the community its first glimpse of the new school, which the headline described as "best of the best." Carty is quoted as saying "Everything is being done to ensure that the school is able to support the students.Classrooms are number one on the priority list."

New E-burg school 'best of the best'

Three students - who will be tour guides - visit the district's new facility in Bushkill

By ANDREW M. SEDER
Pocono Record Writer

BUSHKILL — Three students got their first glimpse of the inside of the soon-to-open new East Stroudsburg High School-North, and they liked what they saw.

Three juniors, who will serve as tour guides to students and parents at Friday's open house, were given a walk-through by Principal Rick Carty Wednesday morning.

Words like "wow!" "modern" and "spacious" were used as the students walked through the high school portion of the north complex.

Even though workers were still completing the job, and boxes, wires, and tools littered the hallways and classrooms, the students were impressed.

Anne Marie Aponte, 16, said that there's a lot to be done before Monday, but she expects the students to be happy with their new house of education.

"I think that everyone had high expectations. I think they've (school district officials) met them," said Aponte, who lives in Bushkill.

"We have the best of the best," Kim Moucha, 16, said.

She said she expected the new school to be like a maze but found it easier to get around than the high school in East Stroudsburg.

All three students agreed on one aspect.

"The north school is better than the south in almost every way," said Moucha.

"This school is modern, it's up to date. It isn't like the south where due to add-ons (Bunnell building and modulars), things just don't match," said Moucha.

Aponte called the East Stroudsburg school "cruddy" and said that the halls weren't wide enough for students to get to their classes smoothly.

"The south is crowded, and here it won't be. We have a larger building and fewer students," Aponte said.

Among the highlights of the tour were the basketball arena with bleachers on all four sides.

"We might not have the best

See BEST Page A-2

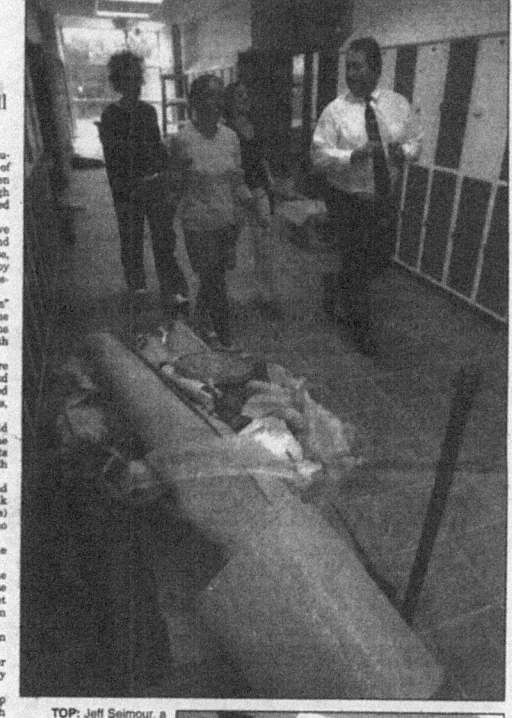

TOP: Jeff Seimour, a technician with Communications Systems of Allentown, works with wiring at the school.

ABOVE: Students, from left, Marlaina Geffers, Anne Marie Aponte and Kim Moucha tour the new school with Principal Rick Carty.

RIGHT: Moucha takes a look at a classroom.

David Kidwell/Pocono Record

The countdown was on. Twelve days until the school year began Being a student-centered administrator, Carty wanted to make the transition as smooth as possible, and on August 23, 2000, three students were given a tour of the nearly finished school. In preparation for an open house to take place on the Friday before the school year's beginning, Kim Moucha, Anne Maria Aponte, and Marlaina Geffers walked the hallways of this building for the first time.

Moucha told *The Pocono Record* that "she expected the new school to be like a maze but found it easier to get around than the high school in East Stroudsburg." On Friday, August 25th, many families with students in grades nine through twelve visited and were guided through the building by Moucha, Aponte, and Geffers, who volunteered to serve as tour guides at the event. When asked how he felt about the school opening, Carty remembers "anxious anticipation."

> [I felt] a little nervous, nervous about everything going well. Because we were basically trying to create a new culture and dis miss all the negativity that was exuded at many of the board meetings prior to us opening. As a staff, we got together and we wanted to make that a great school, we wanted to make the students feel very comfortable, and we wanted them to know that they would be afforded every opportunity that they were at the original East Stroudsburg High School.

The lyrics of the alma mater proudly proclaim, "Oh with you our honor starts, East Stroudsburg Area North," and on the morning of August 28, 2000, it truly started. On that overcast morning, students boarded their buses which were no longer en route to town, but rather, heading toward Lehman Township. Upon passing Bushkill Elementary School, after a slight curve to the left, and another curve to the right, peeking through the trees was the brand-new East Stroudsburg North Campus. The buses dropped the students off in front of the building, a structure that many students had never before seen, and the 696 students entered into the science wing. "What an exciting time for the kids," Kish remembers. "To see them walk in on that first day, their eyes lit up! They got to see the opening of that new building and were reassured that this is gonna be yours. This your building; this is your new home." "We prepared for it, lining up and greeting the kids," said Wilson. "Greeting those buses and seeing kids get off of them…many of their faces you could read like a book." Tamika Roberts, who was a senior, remembers her first day on the North campus. "We actually had orientation that first day, so we were able to walk around and see what the different wings would be called. It put a lot of our minds at ease." When asked about how he perceived the students' response to the transition, Carty felt that it was not easy at first due to all of the negative perception.

> I believe that once we were able to get in the building and we worked together—the staff and the students worked together—it became very spirited and almost a challenge to some of the students that they were gonna get to do something that not many students ever really get to do, and that's to create their own culture.

The lobby and auditorium, Fall 2000

The first day was just as memorable for the teachers and administration as it was for the students. "The first day of school, I wore my German dress, my *dirndl*," recalls Mathiesen. "I remember thinking, wow, here we go, this is the chance to really establish a good program, a good educational setting. Let's make it fun." "It was largely unfinished when it opened," said Zasada. "They were still in the process of putting in TVs in the rooms at that point. I remember one guy carrying these large TVs up a ladder and putting them on these flimsy stands and strapping them up there with what didn't appear to be a strong strap." Debra Padavano, who was teaching emotional support for the first time, remembers a key interaction with her students that set the tone for the year. "I was telling them the rules, and one kid picked up his desk over his head and said, 'Miss, what would you do if I throw this?' And no educational classroom in the world will get you ready for that day! I just told him, 'If you throw that, you're going to alternative ed. And, by the way, don't touch my posters, don't touch this, don't touch that…' And he put the desk down, and thankfully nobody ever threw anything."

An administrator can plan for any possible scenario, but some are simply impossible to predict, and on the first day, McGovern got to experience a first for him. In the afternoon of the first day, "the students going home was delayed because of geese that landed in front of the buses and they wouldn't move!" recalls McGovern. "And the next day the custodians and maintenance had to come in early because of goose droppings that were just littered all over the sidewalk. It was quite a unique experience." This was the first of many unique experiences that took place that first year.

The new school was exciting but was also cause for nervousness. Early in the first semester, a mother arrived at the North High School to enroll her two sons. "They were from Yonkers, New York," Carty remembers. "She was a nervous wreck, she was so worried about her boys, and I could see the worry in her eyes. I remember saying to her, 'Don't worry about a thing, we'll take good care of your boys.' They were nice kids."

For as nervous as the students and the families were, it can safely be said that the faculty were also nervous and unsure about things. "There were so few students, it was a different world," Green recalls. "Everyone was in amazement. Everyone running around trying to figure out what to do." The layout of the building caused unexpected problems. "The first couple of weeks, everybody was late to class," said Carty. "We had to up the amount of time in between classes." "When they said they were opening up in the fall, the school wasn't really ready for opening," Wilson recalls. "The library surely wasn't. The library was one big empty room when we first opened, as was the intermediate library. So, we were not set up and students didn't have a library to come to in the beginning."

This setback, while frustrating, ended up contributing to the staff getting to know each other a bit better. Wilson, along with the library instructional aide, decided to use the time productively by offering to weed through the hundreds of boxes and find materials for teachers.

"I had friends that would be in classrooms who needed things immediately," Wilson said. "They would ask, "If you're down there, can you look out for this box for me? I remember looking for art supplies. While I knew most of the people, a lot of the staff was new. I got to meet a lot of people." "I remember just trying to find books because everything was scattered," Voglino recalls. "I was on the third floor, and all the supplies and books were on the opposite side of the building. That was interesting, finding stuff all that year. I guess that made a bonding with all the teachers and Mr. Carty, just trying to work together and get stuff running."

A close-knit community soon formed among the staff. Newer teachers, as well as the seasoned teachers alike, quickly noticed the welcoming new community that was taking shape before their eyes. Angeline Lombardo, who was a newly-hired mathematics teacher, remembers liking the newness of the school. "The nice thing about a new school is that the cliques were not formed yet. It was new to the students, too." Green, who had taught in the district for over twenty years by this point, shares his appreciation for the new working environment at North:

> The teachers, the staff, we really all worked together. That was so nice. I always think of the first parent-teacher night that we had to be in school. We got a break for dinner and there's no place to go for dinner in that half-hour or hour they allotted. And we got everyone together and did a covered dish dinner with the custodians, the maintenance men, everyone. The secretaries. We all had dinner together with stuff we had brought together. So, that was so different. It wasn't all these little factions that happen in a school.

It is very easy within any working environment for cliques to form. "We decided at North that we weren't going to develop those cliques," said Mathiesen. "We tried really hard to reach and help out the new guy. It became this sense of 'we're here on this island, alone, together.' And that still has not left." "Everyone really wanted this to be the best school it could be," said Carty. "And that's what

I think made it so special in the early years. Because of the immense challenges to start with, people were willing to help each other out. I think that was the best part of the culture of that school was that people embraced it, and they, over time, embraced the new identity of East Stroudsburg North."

The next several pages comprise a "gallery of firsts": artifacts from the first year at East Stroudsburg High School North.

Timberwolves Chronicle

Spirit Week and Homecoming a Huge Success
By Katie Sibilia
News Staff Writer

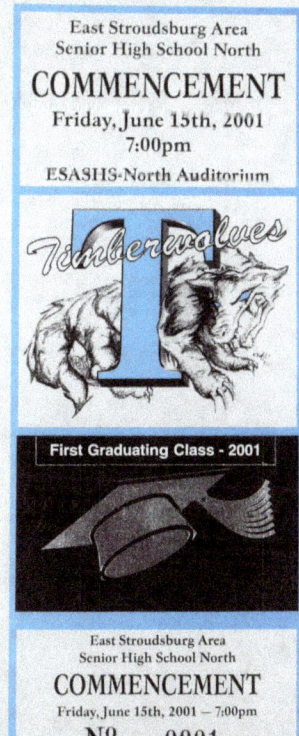

East Stroudsburg Area
Senior High School North

COMMENCEMENT
Friday, June 15th, 2001
7:00pm
ESASHS-North Auditorium

First Graduating Class - 2001

East Stroudsburg Area
Senior High School North

COMMENCEMENT
Friday, June 15th, 2001 — 7:00pm

№ 0001

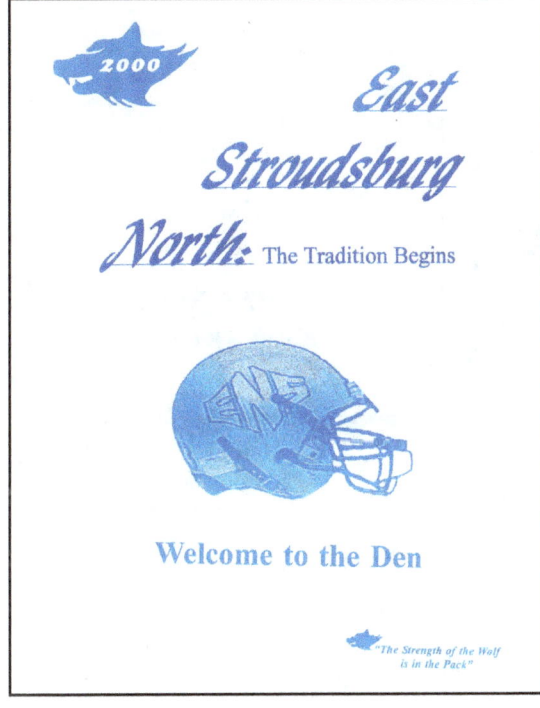

2000

East Stroudsburg North: The Tradition Begins

Welcome to the Den

*"The Strength of the Wolf
is in the Pack"*

93

```
ES Senior High North            1/24/2001        Student Schedule  2000-2001

   ID#          Name                                     Sex   Grade  Hmrm
█████████  ████████████████                            0     11     231

                           Hmrm Teacher- K. HAAS


Crse/Sect   Description          Term   Pds.   Days      Room   Instructor
9981-01     STUDY HALL           1ST    01-01  123456    100
9981-01     STUDY HALL           2ND    01-01  123456    100
477 -01     APPLIED GEOMETRY     SPR.   01-02  123456    231    MS. HAAS
050 -01     PE 11                1ST    02-02  123456           MR. BERKE
051 -01     DRIVER ED/TRAINING   2ND    02-02  123456           MR. BERKE
561 -01     COMPUTER APPL. 2 HON FALL   03-04  123456    207    MS. BEITMAN
253 -02     US HISTORY 3         SPR.   03-04  123456    128    MR. NEVIL
1111-01     LUNCH                FALL   05-05  123456
9980-14     STUDY HALL           3RD    05-05  123456    302
9980-14     STUDY HALL           4TH    05-05  123456    302
1112-02     LUNCH                SPR.   06-06  123456
357 -03     ACAD ENVIR SCIENCE 1 FALL   06-07  123456    115    MS. SOSKIL
9980-16     STUDY HALL           3RD    07-07  123456    302
9980-16     STUDY HALL           4TH    07-07  123456    302
152 -01     ENGLISH 11           FALL   08-09  123456    308    MR. MILSOVIC
632 -02     WOOD TECH 3          SPR.   08-09  123456    112    MR. GREEN
```

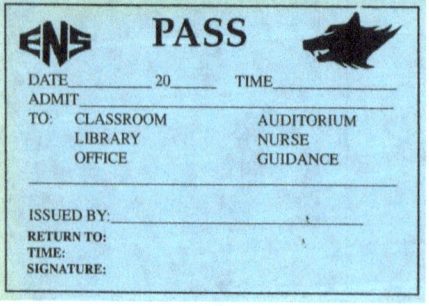

C. Whitmoyer
Rm 224

ⵊⵏⵙ PASS

DATE_____ 20_____   TIME_____
ADMIT_____
TO: CLASSROOM   AUDITORIUM
      LIBRARY   NURSE
      OFFICE   GUIDANCE
_____
ISSUED BY:_____
RETURN TO:
TIME:
SIGNATURE:

EAST STROUDSBURG AREA
SENIOR HIGH SCHOOL
NORTH

HOME OF THE
TIMBERWOLVES

STUDENT – PARENT HANDBOOK
2000-2001

94

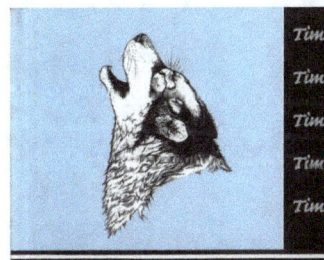

TIMBERWOLVES

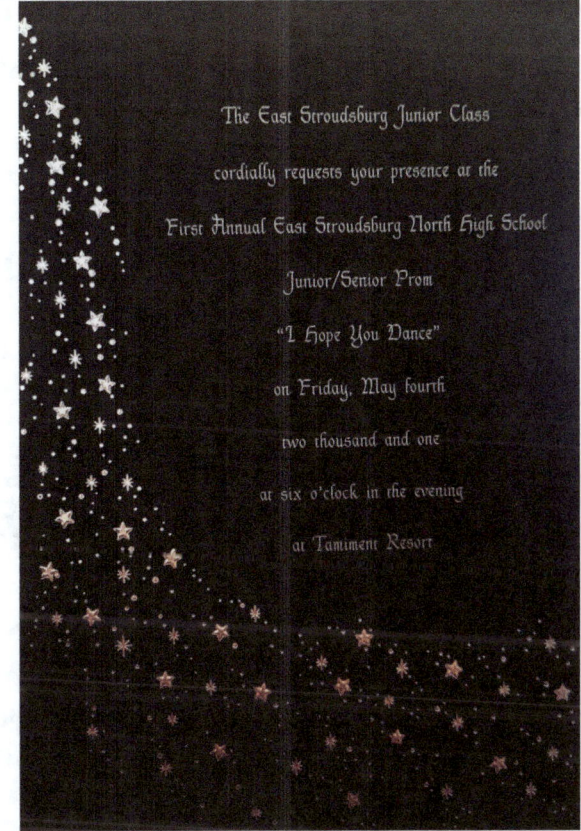

The East Stroudsburg Junior Class

cordially requests your presence at the

First Annual East Stroudsburg North High School

Junior/Senior Prom

"I Hope You Dance"

on Friday, May fourth

two thousand and one

at six o'clock in the evening

at Tamiment Resort

6/14/2001

GRADE: 12   HR: 113   2000-2001

COURSE	DESCRIPTION	TEACHER	1ST	2ND	3RD	4TH	EXAM	FIN	CREDIT
060 -06	PE 12	MS. EICH				S		S	.400
061 -06	HEALTH 12	MS. EICH			94			94	.200
161 -01	ACADEMIC ENGLISH 12	MR. MILSOVIC	93	94			93	93	1.000
260 -01	PSYCHOLOGY	MR. TUDEND	96	94			85	94	1.000
361 -01	ACADEMIC PHYSICS	MR. STINE			85	81	73	82	1.000
450 -02	ADVANCED MATH HONORS	MS. HAAS			94	82	60	85	1.000
600 -02	GRAPHIC ARTS 1	MR. LONG	96	99			95	95	1.000
601 -02	GRAPHIC ARTS 2	MR. LONG			95	98		77	1.000

THIS YEAR TOTAL CREDITS: 6.600

```
* ATTENDANCE        1ST   2ND   3RD   4TH   TOTAL *
*                                                 *
* EXC. ABSENT       .0    .0    .0    .0    .0 *
* UNEX. ABSENT     1.0   1.0   2.0    .0   4.0 *
* TIMES TARDY        0     1     2     5     8 *
* * * * * * * * * * * * * * * * * * * * * * * * * *
```

CREDITS EARNED AS OF 6/14/2001:   30.400
MARKING PERIOD AVERAGE: 87.000 *HONORS*
CUMULATIVE AVERAGE: 87.4476
CLASS STANDING AVG. WEIGHTED: 3.4161
CLASS STANDING: 13

COURSE	TEACHER	COMMENTS
60 -06	MS. EICH	A pleasure to have in class
450 -02	MS. HAAS	Constructively participates in class activities

96

This included not only the people working in the building, but the students who attended there. According to Tamika Roberts, "When people mention school spirit, it's more than just being a Timberwolf. It's how you overcome adversity. And as a class, I think we did that very well." "I remember the students and how they were, and the kindness," recalls McGovern. "And while everyone was little nervous, I just remember how happy they were and how students were excited about the newness of the school." "Once everything settled down and the kids got used to 'this was going to be their home now,' it started to become a community," said Mochan. "That sense of belonging is very strong at North. It was that first year and it hasn't changed." Marcial remembers the degree of involvement that the students had in shaping this community:

> Once the infrastructure was done, there were a lot of notions and ideas — the human structure or the culture. They were given a lot of voice in the culture of what the school would be like as it developed. This notion of 'awesome freedom.' We get to chart our own path and create our own identity. They were given a role in that.

The faculty praise Carty for listening to the student body. "I listened to what they had to say. I learned from them, and hopefully they learned something from me," Carty said. "When you're in charge, it's always good to hear what someone else has to say. As a leader, you have the final say, but people want to be heard." "Mr. Carty was a big believer that for the school to be successful, the students would have to be strong stakeholders in the school itself," said McGovern.

Nace pointed out a very present yet easily overlooked aspect of a school: tradition. "South has tradition, and tradition is awesome. North had no tradition. It was all about starting new and figuring it out and beginning tradition. And that was exciting. Every time we did anything, it was the first time we did anything. There was no past precedent; there was no standard."

As traditions formed, the first year included many of the normal aspects of the high school experience. Following suit of many other high schools, pep rallies and a homecoming celebration were on the agenda. Students quickly got to work in creating Timberwolf artwork and decorating the hallways in blue, black, and silver. The first pep rally came with a lot of excitement. "Everybody was excited to have school spirit," said Roberts. "There was a lot of school spirit because we all loved the school."

As the members of various teams came across the gymnasium floor, one team stood out: the Step Team. "I never knew what a step team was until I saw it at that first pep rally," Zasada recalls. "And I think there was a lot of us that never saw a step team before." Faculty and students alike were impressed by the premiere performance of the step team at the pep rally, many of whom had never seen such an art form before. The first edition of the *Timberwolves Chronicle*, the student newspaper, describes step as "a new wave in school spirit." The students watching their performance responded enthusiastically.

East Stroudsburg North High School's first pep rally

Among the festivities of the pep rally was the announcement of the school's first homecoming court. Since East Stroudsburg North was a new school, it was difficult to anticipate who would be selected as homecoming king and queen. Randy Paolino recalls feeling very surprised when he was named homecoming king.

> That was an honor. I had only lived up there for a couple of years and for me that was a really shocking moment because that role was usually won by the popular kids in school. When I heard that I got nominated, I couldn't even fathom it. I went from nobody knowing who I am to the whole school knows who I am. It was really something I will never forget.

Randy Paolino and Tamika Roberts are named North's first homecoming king and queen

Tamika Roberts, who was named the school's first homecoming queen, recalls the feeling as "exciting."

> I know I keep using the word 'exciting,' but that's the best way I can explain what we were living in the moment. Brand new school, brand new opportunities, and for the student body to nominate me to be the first homecoming queen, it's a rush feeling. It's overwhelming because when you're young and you don't know what's happening, it's overwhelming but it's also a sense of pride and being grateful.

When a typical high school graduate thinks back to their homecoming game, it is often a given that this event takes place on their home campus. Unfortunately, the class of 2001 was not able to experience this in their own field, but rather, in their rival's field.

When the North Campus opened, the high school's football field did not have bleachers. It was decided that all home games would take place at East Stroudsburg High School South's football field. As Carty recalls:

The first year that we competed in football, we shared the stadium at High School South amidst a lot of controversy. It was supposed to be a home game for the North, but at 18 miles away, it wasn't really much of a home contest. And I think the parents felt like they weren't really being treated fairly, and there was a sense of 'we weren't wanted in that stadium.' That was the 'Purple Pit.' The North shouldn't be playing there. They should have their own stadium.

Even prior to the homecoming game, the fall 2000 football season began with a lot of dissatisfaction about the location. "We weren't wanted in the South Stadium," said Dailey. "They didn't want us down there. People were not happy that we were playing down there. Our kids never felt like they had a home." Central administration recognized the frustration expressed by North athletes and their families. Arnold remembers an idea that he proposed at the time to attempt to remedy the situation:

I proposed putting stripes around the stadium on the outer part of the stadium. A purple stripe and a carolina blue stripe. Maybe a 6" stripe, which I thought would be welcoming to the North and it would show that we had both North and South. And we had to buy signage for the scoreboard and press box. That was stuff that would allow us to accommodate which team was playing their home game there that evening. The idea of putting a carolina blue stripe on the South stadium was not well-received.

Though the idea of playing a game at another school's stadium was not appealing, the Timberwolves were eager to start their season. The booster club quickly got to work to raise money for the new teams.

The South High School stadium, set up for a North home game

"I started with a folding table and two buckets out in the field for all the football games," said Krupski. "We set up a table and we started out with soda and chips." "We were new, and we didn't have a single kid on our team who had ever played varsity football before," said Dailey. At the first home game, "I still remember our first touchdown was Victor Clouse, catching a pass from Randy Paolino, and scoring our first touchdown and it was very, very exciting." Accompanying the football team was North's Marching Band, who attempted to keep the mood fun regardless of what was on the scoreboard. "We decided that we were going to keep everything super upbeat," said Pawlikowski. "We played Kool and the Gang's 'Celebration' at every football game, win, lose, or draw."

While the athletic teams were developing a sense of community and pride, similar momentum was taking shape in the music programs. As Pawlikowski worked to develop the Concert Band and Jazz Ensemble, Lisa Yozviak took the reins of the Concert Choir and the Chorale, a select chorus. Additionally, Yozviak and Pawlikowski directed the Seventh- and Eighth-grade Band and Chorus at Lehman Intermediate School.

On December 10, 2000, the community got to listen to the school's musicians for the first time at the Dedication Ceremony of the East Stroudsburg North campus. As part of the program, composer Sherri Porterfield's "Voice of a New Beginning," was an appropriate choice for the first vocal performance and featured the combined talents of choral students in grades six through twelve. "We had strong commitment to the music program that we did to the athletic program and that we wanted to establish successful programs," said Carty. "And I think we had the right people in place to do that. And those programs in the East Stroudsburg School District were always highly regarded and we wanted to continue that."

Choral students in grades six through twelve singing at the dedication ceremony.

At the dedication, faculty members John Johnson and Jeff Nevil, the 2001 class advisor, spoke on behalf of the faculty. Moreover, the student body was represented by Abby Devaney, who served as Secretary of the Student Government in 2000–01. In her own words,

> Education is a community effort. This community's effort has resulted in making the dream of a unique learning atmosphere become a reality. Students want to be here. We have teachers who want to teach and students who want to learn.

Student Government Treasurer, Sarah Wallace, shared a similar sentiment. "'The students and teachers look forward to coming here every day[.] This is the best thing that has happened to me in my life.'" This event also marked the first performance of the school's

East Stroudsburg Area North Alma Mater

Lyrics by Chrissy Contorno, Loren Gentile, Danielle Gioia, Nicole Gioia,
Laura McCalla, Ryan McCarron, Catrina Samonte, Liz Warmbir, David Wertz

Music by Anthony DeAngelis

Copyright © 2002

East Stroudsburg North's Alma Mater was first performed on December 10, 2000

alma mater, which was written by nine student volunteers. Anthony De Angelis, class of 2002, composed the melody, and the song has been performed at every commencement ceremony since.

It was not long before each department began to show their commitment to offering students meaningful learning experiences, both in the classroom and through extra-curricular activities. One of the first student organizations offered was the Foreign Language Club, co-advised by Mathiesen and Jessica Leitzel, who taught Spanish. With a booming membership of thirty-five students, the club hit the ground running in planning language awareness activities and trips to museums, plays, and other cultural activities.

The English Department, in addition to the curriculum for grades nine through twelve, offered courses in Drama and Public Speaking. Early in the school year, the Drama II course staged a production of *Girls to the Rescue*, adapted from a book by Bruce Lansky. This production was overseen by Christine Kropcho, who also advised the student newspaper, *Timberwolves Chronicle*. Students in Eric Anderson's Public Speaking class participated in job shadowing experiences, thereby providing them with real-world application of their course-work. "The first year, the public speaking class only had four kids in it!" said Anderson, "We got sick of just talking to each other after a while, so we did other things as well."

Cross-departmental activities soon took place when Voglino, Marcial, and Tischler arranged an integrated unit about Greece and Rome, including performance of Shakespeare's *The Tragedy of Julius Caesar* and creating representative artwork. Meanwhile, the Wood Technology students produced a wooden hall pass for each classroom, engraved with the school logo and classroom number.

One of the few original wooden hall passes at North that survives today.

When a district splits into two high schools, even in the best of circumstances, it makes sense to share certain resources. Fortunately, technology is often the means to do so. Following the opening of North, the question of how to justify offering two sections of a course came up. Forsyth recalls the solution being found through the technological capacity of the new facility.

> It was a videoconferencing system. We had a system at the High School North, we had a system at the High School South, and for a period of time we shared several classes on a common bell schedule where there wasn't a sufficient enrollment in one building or the other to justify running a class twice.

For many years prior to the North High School opening, an Advanced Placement (AP) English course was offered to qualifying upperclassmen. "I taught English 12 Advanced Placement via Distance Learning when the North campus opened," said Ann Catrillo, an English Teacher at High School South. "Once the teachers were established and North students requested the course, English 12AP was offered as a stand-alone course at the North campus." "It was video and Internet-based at that point," said Forsyth. Kelly Rambone, a paraprofessional, was hired to monitor the students taking AP English via distance learning, which took place in room 100 during the fall 2000 semester. "There was a big screen, a camera and a screen that pulled down," said Rambone. "[The students] did not have computers back then."

The opening of a new school is an exciting, optimistic experience. It can also experience harsh realities. One of the earliest of these was a perceived lack of parental involvement. There were many students at North whose parents worked in New York City, and rather than returning home to Pennsylvania each day, they would opt to spend weekdays in the city and only return on weekends. This placed a heavy burden on the students to also be responsible for their younger siblings. "It made me so very sad," said Wilson, "but those were the realities that quite a number of students had to deal with. They had to come to school, put as positive of a face on as they could."

Carty and the faculty recognized this and attempted to make the students' experiences at school as positive as possible.

Unfortunately, not all situations can be prepared for, such as the death of a student. On December 2, 2000, the Timberwolf basketball team had its first home game in the high school gymnasium, playing against Notre Dame of East Stroudsburg. Excitement was in the air as the Timberwolves ran out onto the gym floor. TV-13 news was broadcasting the game. Carty, Bill David, Mark Brown, and Douglas Arnold were all sitting in the stands.

The first half of the game went normally, and then came halftime. The television broadcast went to commercial. "There was such a long delay at halftime," Arnold recalls. "I didn't know why. I was sitting in the stands, wondering, what's taking so long?" In the visitor's locker room, a Notre Dame High School player named Greg Moyer went into cardiac arrest. The athletic trainer, Chris Rossi, began performing cardiopulmonary resuscitation on Moyer. "We called 9-1-1 almost immediately," said Brown. "There were no paramedics up in Bushkill at the time." With the closest ambulance at the time being in Stroudsburg, paramedics did not arrive at the North High School for forty-five minutes. "The first thing I did was send a security guard out to where the main entrance was to meet the ambulance and bring them to the gym," Carty remembers. "That complex was so big, and where the gymnasium is, it doesn't look like a gymnasium from the outside." All the while, Rossi and Brown performed CPR.

"And another thing...nobody had AEDS," said Brown.

The North Campus was not equipped with automatic external defibrillators. Brown, David, and Carty followed the ambulance to Pocono Medical Center. "I was hoping we'd go in and they'd say, 'Thank goodness we got him here. Things are okay.' We got there and a priest met Billy and I at the door." Sadly, Moyer passed away at the age of fifteen. "The game ended at half-time; you could hear a pin drop," said Kish. "It was awful." "It was the worst feeling I ever felt in my life," said Carty. "I remember walking out of the hospital after they told us that he didn't make it, and I can't even describe what that felt like."

Losing a student is a terrible experience for a school community to endure, and sadly, the student body of East Stroudsburg High School North had to endure this twice within the same week. Several days later, on December 8, 2000, twelfth-grade student Dimon Brown was traveling from the North High School to the Monroe County Area Vocational-Technical School for his afternoon classes, lost control of his car and ran off the road into several trees. He died of blunt force trauma to the head. "That happened year one; that was a big tragedy," recalls Zasada. "That was something we had to deal with, we were still fairly young as a school." A tree was planted on the North campus in Brown's memory.

The first year of the school's history came with sadness, but it also came with happiness. A community was taking shape, and happily, it had become a caring community. "Going up there, the kids were always very nice," said Arnold. Carty and McGovern attempted to be as visible and approachable as possible, attending events and offering to help in any ways that they could. "They kept an upbeat building," Pawlikowski recalls.

In March of 2001, McGovern resigned to accept a principal position nearer to where he lived. Surprisingly, he was not immediately replaced, leaving Carty to oversee the school on his own for the remainder of the year. "It was very hectic, very stressful, especially being the first year that we were there," said Carty. "At the time, the [enrollment] wasn't extremely high but to have no assistance or help was pretty stressful." The teachers recall this period of adjustment. "Finally, at one faculty meeting, [Carty] said, 'Is there anybody in this building who is willing to help me with discipline?' because every single thing was going to him because there was no as-sistant principal," said Darrin Dobrowolski, who taught mathematics.

Maintaining his belief in students being major contributors to the school, Carty turned to his student government for help. "I listened to the student government, and I also had a student advisory committee who I turned to," he said. The physical plant was nearing completion, and while Carty's workload had increased significantly, there were no major problems for the remainder of the first year.

As the school year progressed, the athletic programs continued to work toward excellence. The Timberwolves, be they wrestlers, swimmers, softball players, baseball players, or basketball players, quickly became very dedicated to their sport and proud of their new school. In particular, the girl's tennis team distinguished themselves during their first season, winning six out of eleven matches, earning the Northern Division Title, and qualifying for districts. The coach of their team, Betty Aponte, was new to her role as a varsity coach, and shared the enthusiasm she had for her team with the *Timberwolves Chronicle*:

> Coming into this season, only four of our girls ever even held a racquet. We knew we had a struggle ahead of us, but all the girls worked so hard. While our opponents played with experience, we played with heart.

The soccer team also made commendable progress in its first season. After winning its inaugural game, they won six out of ten games during the season. Coach Arthur Entz viewed the newness of the team as one of the reasons for their success. "Their youth was an asset rather than a hindrance because they will have the opportunity to grow with each other over the next few years," he said.

Carty was a proud spectator of all the teams. Given the mixed opinions that were circulated about the new school, Carty sometimes wondered if the decision to split into two high schools was truly the right decision. One afternoon, he walked out the back doorway of the school, heading toward the athletic fields. He stood there for a moment at the top of the hill, observing various practices taking place. That is when he realized that many of these students might not have had the opportunity to compete in sports at a larger school. It was then when he realized that he was glad that there were now two high schools.

Carty was very proud of the dedication and sacrifices of his students, not only on the athletic fields and in the classrooms, but on the stage. As March of 2001 came to a close, opening night of the school's first spring musical was approaching. In deciding which play to select, Yozviak, the director, reflected on the school's first year for inspiration. The liner notes from the playbill explain the rationale.

> With a central theme of community, Godspell seemed the perfect choice for the first Spring Production of East Stroudsburg High School North. It has been a central goal of our school year to instill feelings of school pride and community among the students, parents, staff, and administrators. I believe that we have witnessed this throughout the entire school, and I have certainly witnessed this throughout the production of Godspell. Many students who had never before participated in a musical production came out to audition and were openly received by our theatrical 'veterans.'

The production was, indeed, a community effort. In the April 6, 2001 edition of *The Pocono Record*, writer Justin Arawjo observed that "the cast is proud of the progress they have made with the show. Poised on the edge of history, they are looking forward to performing." "The work ethic of the students was phenomenal," said Pawlikowski. "The students had this infectious energy that they were going to succeed." "Ideas from students, parents, and teachers were brought together, and the ESAHS North production of Godspell truly represents a fusion of all of our visions and talents," wrote Yozviak.

Following the success of the spring musical, the singers of East Stroudsburg North continued to earn positive acclaim. That same month, students participated in the Pennsylvania Music Educators Association (PMEA) Choral Adjudication Festival, where the Concert Choir earned a rating of "Superior," and the Chorale earned "Excellent." As of this writing, the plaques from this adjudication still hang in the High School's Chorus Room.

With the spring semester winding down, the upperclassmen looked forward to the prom. The prom, which was held at nearby Tamiment on May 4th, graced the theme "I Hope You Dance." "When we got there," Roberts recalls, "there were stars everywhere. We got a candle as a take-home with the theme on it." Bianca Ruffin was North's first prom queen, and Steven Branna was the first prom king.

McGovern (left) and Carty (right) at Prom 2001

Following the prom, the next major event was graduation. Carty, having experience with graduations at the South campus, knew what he *did not* want to happen. "At South, graduating classes would try to outdo the other with ridiculous pranks. I tried to avoid that kind of stuff when we moved North." Keeping true to his philosophy of "spelling out the expectations," Carty called the senior class into the auditorium. He sensed the lack of concern among the student body for how the ceremony would be held. He said, "If I could hand everyone their diploma right now, how many of you would take it and not show up for graduation?" To his disappointment, many hands went up. "Graduation is not about you!" Carty insisted. "It is about your parents, grandparents, the people who watched you grow up since you were a baby. The people who are proud of you. You need to give them a respectable show." The auditorium became silent. "So, for an hour and a half, I think you can manage to do this and make them proud of you. And you want them to be proud of you!" said Carty. "So, there will be no throwing stuff…no shenanigans!"

In the days leading up to the graduation ceremony, Carty wondered if the students would heed his advice. "They were still throwing beachballs and stuff at South," said Carty. "It became 'how can we top what last year's graduating class did? It got out of control. That's not what this is about, they're making a joke about this whole thing."

The seventy-five members of the class of 2001 sit together on the stage

On June 15, 2001, faculty, administration, parents, and loved ones of the class of 2001 poured into North's auditorium. With a class of seventy-five seniors, the First Commencement was able to be held in the auditorium, and to date, is the only graduation to be held there. "It was a nice, small personal experience compared to some of the other graduations," Dobrowolski remembers. As the Concert Band performed "Pomp and Circumstance," the seventy-five seniors field into the auditorium. Roberts, who had served as Vice President of the senior class, recited a poem that she wrote, titled "Over the Years." The Concert Choir, directed by Yozviak, sang a song titled "For Just a Little While," composed by Sally K. Albrecht. The lyrics of the song, capturing the one-year spent on the new campus, read: "For just a little while, we were here together…what a special time it was." "It was a very formal ceremony," said Mathiesen. "What was delightfully missing were the antics you sometimes see at graduations with beach balls and air horns. It was a very formal, very quiet, very dignified ceremony." Sitting on the side-stage with the central administration was Doug Arnold, who described the First Commencement as "very uplifting, and kind of emotional. The year ended it was a successful year in many ways. The kids were very appreciative, and [the ceremony] was absolutely incident-free. It was a very good feeling about what had happened that year and the fact that that was home." The ceremony concluded with a singing of the Alma Mater, sung by the students who wrote it. The class of 2001 is still remembered by the senior faculty as a special group, as Daily recalls. "I remember how close-knit the senior class was. They were given the option of whether they wanted to go to the new school or finish out at South. So [they] made the determination that they wanted to open the new building."

Above and right: Images of Commencement 2001

As a final farewell, Carty shared some caring words that were published in the first edition of the yearbook.

> Congratulations on being the first class to graduate from East Stroudsburg Area Senior High School-North.
>
> As you leave East Stroudsburg North you are beginning a whole new chapter in your life. You have experienced dramatic changes this past school year, and have handled them very well. You will have the memories of a new beginning to take with you and more importantly, the skills and abilities you have acquired here as students. I hope all your experiences here at East Stroudsburg-North were positive.
>
> On behalf of the Administration, Faculty, and Staff, I want to express my appreciation for all the sacrifices you have given to the school. You have left many positive memories and a benchmark for future classes to follow.
>
> I know that all of you possess the qualities which enable you to take advantage of the opportunities and rewards that life has to offer. You are passing through an open door to greater heights, challenges and changes. Change is the law of life and those who look only to the past or present are certain to miss the future.
>
> Remember that learning is a lifelong process…a process that does not end at East Stroudsburg-NORTH. May your future be bright and filled with happiness.
>
> *Richard Carty, Principal*

Group photo of the 2000–2001 faculty and staff

With a year of service as principal now under his belt, Carty could reflect on his approach to administration. "I always tried to praise teachers' positives and not just focus on the negatives," he said. "I wanted to make them feel important." That being said, Carty was not shy of offering criticism when needed. "If I had a nickel for every time I told a teacher, 'It's not about you,' I'd be a millionaire!"

Carty made it a practice to remind teachers that they are there for the students. Faculty members at the North High School quickly began to favor Carty's leadership. "I think he was a very good leader, he had a good vision," recalls Melissa Sherman, who taught chemistry when the building opened. "He listened to his staff; he was willing to take your suggestions." "He was a 'player's coach,'" said Frable. "He would never embarrass you or come down on you if you were lacking in the classroom or needing assistance. He never made you feel like you weren't worthy. It's really hard to find someone in a position like that nowadays that really can communicate the way he does and make you as comfortable as he has." "He was exactly what that building needed at that time," said Dailey. Despite the many challenges encountered during the first year, Carty succeeded in developing a close staff and a respectful relationship with them.

As he prepared for the 2001–2002 school year, Carty anticipated a major theme being growth. Since the class of 2001 had the option of not attending the North High School, which many students took advantage of, the incoming freshmen class would be considerably larger than the class that graduated. This population growth prompted the need for additional faculty. Ten new teachers joined the faculty in 2001, five of which were replacements of teachers who left, and five who were new positions.

Several of the new faculty members had moved into the high school after teaching at Lehman Intermediate for the first year. The most notable new addition to the North High School was Patricia Mulroy, who was selected to replace McGovern as the assistant principal. Mulroy, who had known Carty for many years prior, appreciated the work he had done to establish the North High School.

Patricia Mulroy, Assistant Principal

"[Carty] had done a lot for the morale and positive support that was going in there," said Mulroy. "He was really about giving the students a voice, so I was excited to go and learn with him." Being fairly new to working as an administrator, Mulroy appreciated the mentoring that Carty provided. "If I had a question, he was really great about showing me the ropes and teaching me how to go through those processes. I learned a lot about being a student-centered leader from him because he was really about the kids." "It was a pretty easy working relationship between the two of us," Carty recalls. "Pat was really laid back, very relaxed about things," said Nace. "She was a very warm person, she cared about the kids, she was very fair," said Padavano. "The kids seemed to respond to her because she's real," said Wilson. Carty and Mulroy worked together for the next two and a half years.

School administrators begin a school year with hopes for as smooth of an experience as possible, and do their best to create a safe, controlled environment. The reality, unfortunately, is that the outside world bears heavily on the school. This is especially true in the event of a disaster, and on Tuesday, September 11, 2001, the hallways of East Stroudsburg North were filled with emotion and panic.

If you ask anybody about September 11th, they will likely be able to tell you a vivid story of what they remember from that tragic day. Just after 9 a.m., Dailey was standing at the end of the physical education hallway and looking out the window, taking notice of the crystal clear weather. "Holly Eich came out of her office and told us that a plane hit the World Trade Center," said Dailey.

At the time, not all classrooms at East Stroudsburg North had Internet access. Rumors began to spread throughout the building and teachers wanted to know what was going on. "I had a desktop computer in my classroom at the time and I don't think I had Internet access on that computer," said Trish Leibig. "I couldn't get on the Internet in my classroom so I went down to the library and you couldn't get on any of the news sites." In the office, Carty and Mulroy began to notice a high frequency of parents arriving to pick up their children. "Before it hit the news, people were aware of it, and the people who were aware of it were parents who had relatives who were working at the World Trade Center," said Carty. "There were parents coming into the building, wanting to take their kids out." "We shut down the TVs and the news," said Mulroy. "In hindsight, maybe it wasn't the best thing to do, but at the moment we didn't want someone to find out on TV that they had lost a parent or an aunt or an uncle or somebody that they knew."

The teachers remember trying to support the students as best as they could. "I just remember watching the kids' realities melt," remembers Pawlikowski. "And then the personal situation of, 'my dad works in that building.' That was really the end of our teaching day that day. It was more about seeing who needed what, making a thousand phone calls." "It was terrible, I was hoping that none of my students' relatives were there, because I knew a lot of the parents would commute back and forth to the city," said Lombardo. "They opened up all the phone lines so kids could get out on every single phone line," Mulroy recalls, "so eventually everybody could figure out if their parents were okay."

As the school day progressed, the question of where will students go if they return home to an empty house became a concern. "JTL was the place where if there was nobody home, the kids went there and stayed there late at night until someone picked them up," said Padavano. "I can remember that day in the building was very chaotic because there were people that had relatives that worked there," said Carty. "We were lucky, I don't think we had anybody who directly lost a parent," said Mulroy.

With the start of a fall semester comes the start of football season, and once again, home games at North were a popular topic of discussion. The school district realized that scheduling North's home games at the South's stadium was no longer an option.

Football Game Day Program
for the 2001 season

"I remember one time the North played a home game down there and [the players] were on the bus to leave…and they were already changing the signage over!" said Arnold. "It was like, 'here's your hat, what's your hurry? Goodbye!' I think that upset some folks, too. At least let us leave and then you can change it back over." Getting the North High School's football field ready to host games was a challenge. "We didn't have a press box, we just didn't have things in place yet," David recalls. "I think it was as simple as how do we get people to buy tickets?"

Movable bleachers were assembled around the field, however, this offered only limited seating for spectators. "If anybody stood up in front, you couldn't see unless you were on the third or fourth row… and there weren't many rows to those bleachers," recalls Arnold.

So, in typical North fashion, the staff, students, and parents came together and devised solutions. "I remember our first press box was a scaffold that we put up on the road that looked down on the field," said David. Preparations for the football field soon found their way into faculty lesson plans when Green's "Wood Construction Technology" course decided to build a concession stand. "That concession stand was a great project," said Green. "Why wasn't that even considered? Why did they build that field and not put a concession stand in? So, that was the solution. And it's a great builder for students to be involved in that kind of stuff." "It's a prime example of 'you can make do,'" said Dailey. "If you get creative and you get people who want to help, you can make it happen."

Perhaps playing on their home field was motivation for the Timberwolves, who, in their second season, saw considerable improvement as a team. Their motto, "0-10, never again," was echoed among the staff and players. The 2001 football season also included its homecoming game, which allowed the student body to get creative with floats for each class. The theme: children's television shows. While the setup of the football field and lack of seating were not ideal, clearly the North community was happy to no longer share a field with a rival school.

Carty crowns the 2001 homecoming king at the North High School field.

Technological progress began to flourish at East Stroudsburg North during the second year. In the mathematics department, Dobrowolski led his Multimedia II class through the development of the school's first custom-designed Web site. Several teachers developed home pages for themselves on the district's domain, which had recently been renamed "esasd.net." "There was a period of time," recalls Forsyth, "where it was 'the thing to do.' We gave teachers access to Web authoring within a particular location in their building where they could publish their bio and so forth."

Welcome to Mr. Dobrowolski's Virtual Classroom

I teach the following classes at the East Stroudsburg High School North Campus: Computer Literacy & Usage, Multimedia, AP & Honors Calculus, and Computer Methods and Programming Honors.

Computer Literacy & Usage - In the class, students learn the basic computer programs; this includes Microsoft Office 2001, Appleworks 6.0, and Hyperstudio 4.2.

Multimedia -This class is reserved for Juniors and Seniors only. In this class, students learn Hyperstudio in depth, Flash 5, and iMovie 2.3. It is a good idea to take Computer Literacy & Usage first, but it is not a requirement. Students will create interactive presentations using Clipart, Animations, Sounds, Music, and much more. They will also work in groups to create several movies using Digital Video Cameras and iMovie. Digital Cameras, and scanners are also used.

AP & Honors Calculus - This class is for those students who excelled in Advanced Math Honors. For AP Calculus, students should have at least scored an 85% for the year in Advanced Math Honors to take the class. For Honors Calculus, students should have at least scored a 75% in Advanced Math Honors. AP tests are offered in the spring. Students who score well on the AP exam will receive college credit. **STUDENTS NEED TO CONTACT THE COLLEGE THAT THEY ARE PLANNING TO ATTEND TO FIND OUT WHAT SCORE THE NEED TO ACHIEVE ON THE EXAM IN ORDER FOR IT TO COUNT AS A COLLEGE COURSE!

Use the below bulleted links to link to other places within this webpage for more information on your class:

- Homework/Project Update
- Special Happenings in the School/Classroom
- Links to Websites that extend classroom learning

PA MATHEMATIC LEAGUE CONTESTS - Open to any student who wants to participate in the contest. The are a total of six contests involving six questions each. The students who participate will miss 45 minutes of there 1st Block class on the following Dates: October 30, December 4, January 8, February 4, March 4, and April 9. Topics will range from Algebra 1 to Precalculus. The top 5 scores at each contest get sent to the state for the "Team Score".

One of the first faculty Web pages authored at the North High School

Computer education was expanding, as students could take courses in digital graphic design, Microsoft Office applications, Web design, computer literacy, and computer programming.

The Technology Education Department rolled out a new course, TV and Video Production, in 2002. Among the many facilities in the school was a Media Center that housed three editing rooms and a small television studio. "We lacked some of the equipment to get it started [earlier]," said Carty. "That was also one of the areas that wasn't exactly ready when we moved into the building."

The beginning of "live" (closed circuit) daily television broadcasts began in April 2002. Every morning at 9:00, teachers turned on channel 20 for "North News," a ten-minute program that featured morning announcements, sports scores, and a weather report.

Clockwise: The media classroom; an editing room with iMac computer; the opening title for "North News" in spring 2002; Carty on "North News"

"We were involved with the design of the studio," recalls Forsyth. "We had a coaxial cable system running through that entire building. We had the ability to originate two programs outside of the actual studio that could be brought back and mixed into the studio broadcast." "That was Craig Long who ran that studio, he did such a good job of moving people through," said Mulroy. "I think they even started videotaping games before that was a thing. They would do that and then show some highlights. It was really fun." "And we were very thankful for [Long's] commitment to that program because it really grew over the next couple years," said Carty. Daily production continues today, now under the new title of "North Drive Live," which includes YouTube streaming which was not possible in 2002.

Technology was being used in the North High School for creative expression, communication, and problem solving. Now more aware than ever of the technological capabilities available to them, Carty was curious to see how it could make processes easier. Often one of the most dreaded chores an educator must complete is the calculation of final grades. At the time, the teachers had to submit their final grades on computer response forms. "We had these giant Scantrons that were 14x18" that we had to fill out for every class," Dobrowolski remembers. "It was this weird-sized paper and we had to go through and fill out…if it was a 79%, we had to fill in the bubble of the 7, then the 9. It was very time-consuming." Mulroy remembers a particularly tedious experience with the generating of report cards.

Mr. Carty and I had to take down stacks and stacks and stacks of those data cards…and we had to run every one through the Scantron on a Friday night! (There had been a mistake). It was one of those old mainframe computers. We had to go down and put those computer cards into the old computer and then the report cards got spit out so that we would have report cards for Monday morning. We'd put [the Scantrons] in and then we had to sit there, it obviously had to "bake" the information…and they printed out and they got delivered to us.

Recognizing the archaic nature of this process, Carty found a computer program that would permit teachers to submit their grades digitally instead of needing to use a paper form. "It was picked by Mr. Carty, and we used it at the North High School, but it wasn't district wide," said Dobrowolski. "The beginning of technology is really hard in the classroom," said Mulroy. "Those were painful years! It was hard on teachers; it took more time." Within a year, the district purchased LetterGrade, an online grading system developed by TENEX.

Outside of class, student participation in clubs and sports continued to be strong. Recognizing a commitment to business education, a chapter of the Future Business Leaders of America (FBLA) was established during the second year.

The Girls' Tennis Team completed their season with a score of 9-4 in regular season play, and, proudly, beat the South High School 4-3.

The Timberwolves Soccer Team was only one win short of qualifying for districts, and in cross country, Jason Alers became the first North athlete to qualify for states.

While the Timberwolves were showing excellence on the field, the music programs were achieving excellence on the stage. The school's second musical, *Footloose*, received a positive response from the community. Around the same time, Pawlikowski was eager to develop new traditions for the band program and decided to audition for Disney's "Magic Music Days."

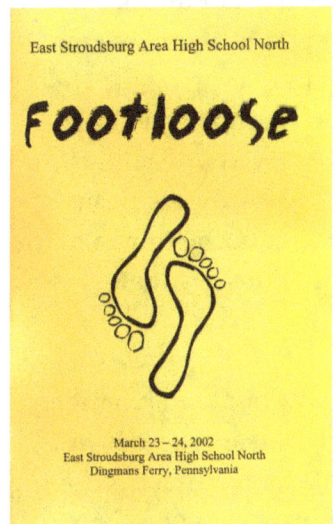 

Left to right: The program for Footloose; *Pawlikowski with the 2001–02 bands.*

"I wanted to take our Band to Florida," said Pawlikowski. "I remember we practiced, we had to do an audition tape. We marched around that front cul-de-sac of the school about seven times as we videotaped us playing 'The Electric Slide.' We kept all of our marching music popular and upbeat, and we got in!"

On June 5, 2002, East Stroudsburg North held its Second Commencement. The class of 2002, which was considerably larger than the class of 2001, would not fit comfortably in the auditorium with their guests. Instead, the graduation was held in the gymnasium. Upon taking the stage, Carty looked out at the 168 graduates and tears filled his eyes. "You will always have a special place in my heart," he said.

"I am just so proud of you." As a finishing touch, the Concert Choir sang an arrangement of Dr. Seuss' "Oh the Places You'll Go," written by 2002 graduate Anthony DeAngelis.

"The class of 2002 will leave me with many fond and positive memories of a responsible, talented, and enthusiastic class that took great pride in their school," wrote Carty in his yearbook message. "I hope all your experiences here were memorable ones."

Many students do not realize that the adults in the school are often students, too. Whether pursuing additional certification or working to maintain their education certificate, it is not uncommon for teachers and school administrators to take graduate courses while working full-time. Carty was no exception to this.

While coaching, planning and opening a new school, and then serving as its principal, Carty was enrolled at Marywood University, located in Scranton. With online education being only in its infancy at the time, Carty's classes took place on campus, requiring him to drive to Scranton once or twice each week. Carty found his graduate classes to be very enlightening.

I took a graduate class where we had to write our own biography. It wasn't until I did that until I realized why I was where I was. My teachers — Mr. Jones and Mr. Houston — had so much influence on me in a positive way and I wanted to impart that on others. I realized that I treated people the way I did because that's what they are going to remember. So, the professor says, 'I want everyone to write down something that they remember about their education. It could be elementary school, junior high, or high school. I want you to write something down that you remember.' Every single male in that class wrote something that happened to them that was negative. The only students in that class who wrote something positive about their education were the female students in that class. (I wrote about the 'the memory board.') The reason he did that was to help us think about how do you want to be remembered. You guys only remember the negative things, so, do you want to be remembered for negative things? If kids are that impressionable, why would you give them some thing negative to remember you about? That's how much influence you have on students. And I'm thinking to myself, 'Now, why would I want to be remembered like that?' That had a lasting impression on me. I used to try to teach the teachers that, too.

Often how somebody is remembered comes from not only what they say, but how they are made to feel. "In a lot businesses and a lot of schools, it's 'us vs. them.' That's the way it is. In my mind, that's not how it should be. This is exactly the way I viewed everything: we're a team. I always felt like a school was a team."

As a principal, Carty did not view education as black and white, believing that every case should be dealt with individually. "Let's say you did something, and it was the first time you ever did it. I think I should treat you differently than someone who's been in my office ten times for the same reason. I disagree with 'you do this, you get that.'" Carty always attempted to figure out the root of a student's behavior before imposing consequences. "Teachers were always complaining about this one girl," Carty recalls. His response was, "do you know anything about

Richard Carty at his desk, fall 2002.

this girl? Well, maybe you should learn about her life because it's amazing she shows up to school every day!" Carty took the time to listen to this student, who was willing to talk openly to him. One day, the student was intercepted at the bus stop when she put a knife to someone's throat. Upon entering Carty's office, he asked her, "Do you have anything on you that you shouldn't have?" She answered him honestly, "Yes, in my purse." Carty said, "Dump your purse on my desk," and the knife came out. When he asked her why she had the knife, she explained that her mother had given her money to score drugs for her, and the person stiffed her. Her mom was putting pressure on her to get the money back, so in frustration, she took a knife to his throat. "I never saw her again. It was sad because there were parts of her you wanted to root for and wanted her to make it," said Carty. "How do you make it when you got that kind of stuff going on at home?"

The 2002–2003 school year saw more growth at East Stroudsburg North. Following the terrorist attacks of September 11th, 2001, many more families moved out of New York and bought homes in the Poconos, many of which were within the East Stroudsburg Area School District's territory. Some families stayed, while others moved to other parts of the region. To accommodate the growing population four additional faculty members were hired, and the bell schedule was revised to include four lunch periods, totaling ten periods in a school day. With the rapidity of change came the side-effect of transience. As Marcial explains:

> As the years went on, I think part of the problem wasn't the quality of who was up there…it was just the idea of transience. There was a lot of in and out in the faculty and the administration there. The students were given a good say in terms of developing the culture there, but that culture was a transient culture. Not just for students but for teachers and administrators. It's hard to develop roots and feel those connections when you have a structure of people coming and going so quickly.

Fortunately, a feeling of belonging had been well established by this point, and new additions to the student body were generally welcomed with acceptance. In early 2003, planning began for a community event that was intended to unify the students and the larger community. "Relay for Life," a twenty-four-hour fundraising event for the American Cancer Society, was scheduled to take place at East Stroudsburg North. Students, faculty, and community members eagerly signed up to participate, forming teams and donating in honor or in memory of a loved one who was affected by cancer. The event became a very memorable end to the spring semester, both for its honorable cause and the well-intended mischief that often took place. Carty had the misfortune of being the brunt of several pranks over the years. "Mr. Carty was laying in his tent...and we would put toilet paper all around his tent to try and lock him in that way! We used to have so much fun!" said Padavano.

Not all pranks, unfortunately, could be chuckled about. Several members of the class of 2003 learned this when they took a "senior prank" a bit too far. A group of three students decided to steal signage and decorations from three local businesses and "decorate" the entrance to the North campus with their loot. "The kids couldn't keep it to themselves, they were bragging, so it wasn't hard to figure out," said Carty.

Mulroy quickly found the three students and proceeded with discipline. Given the severity of the situation, Mulroy informed the three students that they would not be permitted to walk in their graduation. At the time, Carty was downtown at a meeting. While driving back to the North High School, Carty received a call from Mulroy who informed him of what had transpired. During that conversation, the parents of the three students were calling the school. Carty advised Mulroy, "Don't take those calls yet, I'll think of something. Let them sweat a little bit." Carty realized that the students could care less about attending the graduation ceremony, but did the parents, grandparents, and loved ones deserve to be punished?

Carty arrived in his office and there were three phone messages waiting for him. He returned the calls of the anxious parents and said very calmly,

This is what we're gonna do. I'm gonna allow them to walk in graduation and I want each of them to write three letters to the businesses where they stole these things. Keep in mind, the businesses have every right to press charges. They are going to walk in graduation but there will not be a diploma in their folder. The only ones who will know that are me, you, and your son.

Carty also insisted that the three students return to the High School at 8:00 the next morning to help the custodians clean up from the commencement ceremony. "Since we had to clean up their mess, they will help us," he said. "Once they finish cleaning up, we will have a 'special ceremony' in my office." Fortunately, none of the businesses chose to press charges and all stolen property was returned. "One of the kids went to the businesses in person and apologized," said Carty. "I did not ask him to do that."

One might quickly assume that students are the only ones in a school community who need to learn lessons, however, it is possible that the students can also be the ones to offer lessons. Lessons in trust and capability are sometimes offered to adults who fear that the students may not be mature enough to act appropriately in certain situations. A prime example of this came in 2003 when East Stroudsburg North staged *Chicago* as its spring musical.

Program cover for Chicago.

"There was a little controversy because it was a play that had some adult overtones to it," said Carty. "I read the script and was assured by the director that everything would be in good taste, and I believe it was." "I think sometimes people don't think that you can trust young people with hard content and hard concepts," said

Mulroy. "But I think young people are way more capable, and they know way more than we give them credit for." An eyewitness to this production was Paul Bakner, who replaced Pawlikowski as the band director in 2002. "Lisa had a real talent for having these visions and seeing what North was actually able to accomplish in that early stage, and she really brought the best out of these kids."

Chicago was not only a spectator experience for Carty, but an acting one! "They even wrote me a part in that play! It was just a cameo appearance. I think I ended up getting killed off in the story." So much for a second career in theatre.

East Stroudsburg North was growing very quickly. The population was growing, classes were becoming very crowded, and while study hall offered a temporary solution, it brought a new raft of issues. At the May 7, 2003 meeting of the school board, Carty pointed out that nearly 200 students, which was roughly twenty percent of the student population at the time, were assigned to study halls throughout the school day. The school's two large-group classrooms were already overpopulated, so study halls were now being held in the cafeteria and auditorium. Additionally, due to the lack of furniture to accommodate such high numbers of students in the study halls, many students had to sit on the floor during these ninety-minute study halls.

Carty also voiced a need for additional teachers. Despite hiring five additional teachers for the 2002–2003 school year, class sizes were exceedingly high. Classrooms intended to house twenty-five students were, in some cases, holding thirty-six students. Carty requested the board to approve nine new teaching positions and an additional assistant principal position for the upcoming school year.

The crowding of the school was quite evident at the 2003 graduation. "The third year it was getting pretty crowded in the gymnasium," said Carty. "We were only able to afford each student a couple of tickets for their parents and families to attend graduation." The Third Commencement, despite being crowded, was yet another special evening for the graduating Timberwolves. The chorus again sang De Angelis' arrangement of "Oh, the Places You'll Go," and the class treasurer, Jaclyn Bigio, recited a poem. After the ceremony, a familiar face approached Carty.

Everett Alers, who three years prior, moved to the area, and had now graduated. "His mother was so happy that her sons had done so well. I told her, 'I loved watching him play sports, he was such a good athlete, but more than that, your son is a very good person.' That means a lot to a parent."

With three years in the books, East Stroudsburg High School North had seen growth, change, victory, and most importantly, resilience. A new tradition started where the graduating class purchased a gift for the school, several of

The gift from the class of 2003.

which are still in the building. The class of 2003's contribution was a digital marquee, which still hangs in the cafeteria today.

With the beginning of the 2003–2004 school year came even more progress. Fortunately, Carty's request for nine additional teaching positions was approved. In addition to these nine new teachers, seven teachers decided to leave during the summer of 2003. Thus, sixteen new teachers joined the faculty that fall.

Additionally, Carty's request for a second assistant principal was approved, and West Chester University graduate Hugh Braun was selected for the position. Braun had previously served as a physical education teacher for students with special needs, and when interviewed by the student newspaper about why he decided to apply for the job, he responded "...because it's a beautiful area and it offers you the best diversity you can have."

The administrative trio was now in place and ready to address the growing population. The first change was an expansion of the course offerings, specifically offering half-credit electives. "The first couple of years we had quite a few students sitting in study halls," said Carty. "And the only way to eliminate the number of students sitting in study halls was to offer more electives. And we really felt like it was important that they have as many classes and as many opportunities as they could and not be in study halls."

A district-wide change came into effect that year when the "Academic Track" of core courses was retitled "College Preparatory," to encourage more students to consider attending college upon graduation from high school.

Extracurricular activities continued to expand, with new clubs such as the Latin Dance Club, Math and Computer Club, and a chapter of the Rotary Club now offered to students. The student newspaper, which began as the *Timberwolves Chronicle* and was later *The Howl*, was now in its third iteration. Boasting its new name, *The Wolf Pack Chronicle*, student participation in the newspaper was steadily increasing. The creative contributions of students across the school were also increasing, with student-made digital graphics appearing on the covers of the handbook and the program of studies.

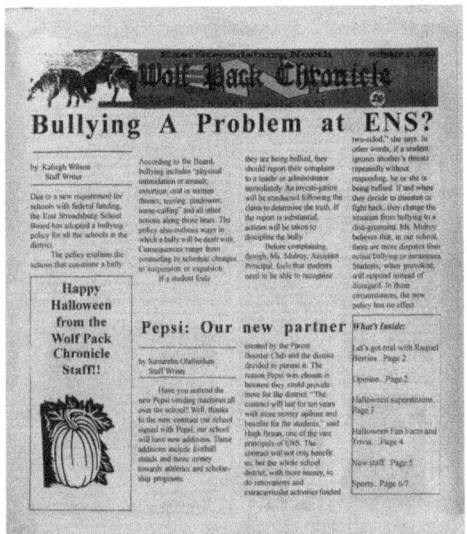 

Left to right: The Wolf Pack Chronicle in 2003; The Program of Studies cover featuring student-made digital graphics

Progress can often become expensive, and East Stroudsburg North's athletic program was no exception to that. The lack of a stadium at the football field had continued to be a point of contention for parents and students, and by 2003, had reached its boiling point. "There was a lot of participation at school board meetings over that subject," said Carty. "When they built the school, for whatever reason, they built the field, they put a scoreboard there, and they put lights there, but they never put bleachers or a concession or bathrooms," said Dailey. Carty recalls that "several of the North parents came to a board meeting and requested that they get their own stadium, which at the time, was not affordable for the district." Among those parents was Diane Krupski. "[Krupski] had brought up the idea of seeking corporate sponsorship, and at that time particularly she had mentioned Coca-Cola. The board said 'sure, go ahead, see what you can find,'" said Dailey. Eventually, the school entered into a ten-year exclusive beverage contract with Pepsi, which included a $100,000 bonus. To some, this probably sounds like a happy resolution, but unfortunately, it was not.

At the December 15, 2003 board meeting, conflicting opinions about how the money should be spent ate much of the meeting time. Several of the board members felt that the money should be equally divided between the North and the South high schools. Being at an impasse, the committee tasked with allocating the funds tabled their proposal for one month. At the next meeting of the school board, six board members voted against using $116,000 toward the construction of the bleachers. Community participation about the Pepsi contract became increasingly vocal over the next year, with some parents speaking during meetings while others sent letters to the local newspaper.

While frustration increased about the football field, work continued in the school building. In January of 2004, another noticeable change occurred when Patricia Mulroy accepted the principal position at Bushkill Elementary School, following Joseph Yanek's departure. Replacing Mulroy was Carolyn Krotowski, who, like Mulroy, had a background in physical education. "The faculty was amongst the best faculty I've ever worked with," Krotowski recalls. "Very cordial, very family oriented and community based."

It is important to remember that the North Campus community includes not only the high school, but also the neighboring Lehman Intermediate and Bushkill Elementary Schools. An excellent example of this community took place in April 2004 when the fourth spring musical, *The Wizard of Oz*, took the stage. Performing alongside the high schoolers were students from Lehman Intermediate, Bushkill and Middle Smithfield Elementary Schools, some as young as eight years old. "There have been many challenges in making this huge classic theater production come to life on our stage," wrote Yozviak. "Elaborate set requirements, diverse costuming, and large cast size are among the many qualities that separate this show from our previous North Campus productions." The show also made use of multimedia, computerized lighting setups, and featured a pit orchestra. "Our outstanding students and parents have proven that East Stroudsburg High School North is diverse enough to do everything from modern Broadway to classic MGM theater," said Yozviak.

Left to right: Photography and the program from The Wizard of Oz

The class of 2004 had witnessed the North High Schools' doors open, the population exceeding a thousand students, and everything in between. The outgoing seniors expressed their appreciation by purchasing carpets for the school entrance and a "wolf shrine" that still sits in the lobby. A proper send-off for this class was in order, but Carty knew that another graduation in the gymnasium would not be possible. Meanwhile, just three miles from campus sat the Mountain

Gifts from the class of 2004

Laurel Center for the Performing Arts. This venue, constructed at what had been the Unity House Resort for the International Ladies' Garment Workers Union, now featured an amphitheater with 2,500 seats. By early 2004, the facility was constructed but not quite ready for occupancy. This gave Carty an idea. "I thought that would be a perfect place to hold graduation. If we could pull that off, we wouldn't have to play the weather issues with graduation. And, it was a big facility, we would be able to hold more people, more family and friends could attend graduation."

Carty contacted the director of the venue, Richard Bryant, who was agreeable to Carty's idea, but pointed out that much needed to be done to open the venue. "Nothing would be better than to have the opportunity to be able to have an entire school full of advocates to state this institution is part of the community, but have got to make sure it will work and be safe and secure and that the building can be put back on line, so to speak," Bryant said to *The Pocono Record*. "We had to go through a lot to get the building open to hold graduation, but we felt it would be a worthwhile cause," said Carty. Not only would this be a laborious task, but an expensive one, requiring $15,000. "We had nine days to pull this off!" recalls Carty.

Raising such a large amount in less than two weeks, while carrying out the usual end-of-year responsibilities of the school, was a tremendous challenge. Knowing he would need help, Carty contacted the state representative, who he had formerly coached in baseball, Kelly Lewis. "I said, 'Let me see what I can do,'" said Lewis. "So, I talked to the people at Mountain Laurel…There were some things that they were never able to purchase that would make it work as a high school graduation site." Lewis contacted numerous business owners across the school district's geographic territory, "almost all of them were East Stroudsburg High School graduates that appreciated that were trying to get it open for the graduation," said Lewis. "Kelly Lewis did much of the legwork," said Carty. "He was very instrumental in talking to local businesses and local politicians. And we were able to raise the money that we needed to get that building opened."

Work quickly began to set up for the Fourth Commencement ceremony. "When I first walked into the back of the hall to set up for graduation," Bakner remembers, "I was floored at this amazing facility that we were able to use for graduation. There were logistical issues that we had to overcome — moving the equipment from the high school to Mountain Laurel — but that was a small price to pay for having such a great venue." The 220 graduating seniors were bussed over to the center for graduation practice, and despite the lack of familiarity with the venue, everybody figured out what to do and prepared to put on a good show for their families. "Our graduations were always dignified, and we were always really proud of that, and Rick Carty started that," said Mulroy.

Just after 4:00 p.m. on June 11, 2004, the graduates filed in. After introductions from the class president, and a poem reading from the class treasurer, Carty approached the microphone. "Welcome parents, family, friends, faculty, administrators, school board members, and graduates to the fourth commencement of the East Stroudsburg Area Senior High School North. This commencement is very special since this class is the first class to complete all four years at East Stroudsburg Area Senior High School North." The amphitheater filled with applause. After thanking the many individuals who contributed to the ceremony, Carty addressed the families of the graduates.

East Stroudsburg Area Senior High School North

DINGMANS FERRY, PENNSYLVANIA

The Fourth Commencement

FRIDAY, JUNE ELEVENTH
TWO THOUSAND AND FOUR

MOUNTAIN LAUREL ARTS CENTER
FOUR O'CLOCK IN THE AFTERNOON

Richard Carty speaking at the 2004 commencement ceremony

I would I remiss if I we did not begin the ceremony with a heart-felt congratulations to the parents who have raised these young people to value the education offered to them. And have supported their children throughout four emotionally demanding years. To the graduates, we learned moving this graduation to The Arts Center in just nine days, the power of what people can do when they work together. As graduates, what I am wishing for you, is that you do for the world and those in need that you come in contact with, what your alma mater has done for you. Be true to yourself and give of that truth to others. Impart knowledge, wisdom, and your best judgment, but most of all, acknowledge that service to others in life is your real treasure. A treasure beyond all imaginable. A treasure multiplied by the number of lives that you will touch. I wish this for each and every one of you. Thank you.

Sitting on the stage near Carty was Sue Wilson, who was the class advisor. In years past, the class advisor did not offer remarks at graduation, but Wilson did not let that stop her. "I wanted those kids to know that they were cared about, they would be thought of, and that they made a difference," Wilson remembers. "And I remember saying, 'I don't think anyone would mind if I said a few parting words.' And I did, and I'm so glad I did, because I saw some of my kids start to cry, and it was honestly one of the best pieces of my life so far. There was a lot of love exchanging in that air." The 2004 graduation went smoother than expected, and for the next eleven years, East Stroudsburg North's graduations took place at the Mountain Laurel Center.

With a new school year often comes new accountabilities, and in the early 2000s, these accountabilities presented themselves in the form of standardized tests. As a result of the No Child Left Behind Act of 2001, each state required the administration of standardized achievement tests to each student within a particular grade. In Pennsylvania, students in grades five, eight, and eleven were required to earn a proficient score on the Pennsylvania System of School Assessment (PSSA) examinations. East Stroudsburg North's math scores were below the state standard and the school needed to address this. Beginning in the fall of 2004, students were tested using the Measures of Academic Progress (MAP) testing program to determine remedial needs and predict their success on the PSSA examination.

Several non-credit remedial courses in math and reading were offered to students who had a study hall in the schedule, and daily practice problems were integrated into teacher's lesson plans.

Though standardized test preparation was a high priority, Carty made sure that the total academic and extracurricular program was not diminished. Electives remained available for students and club participation continued to be strong. With increasing student interest in computers, particularly desktop publishing, came the production of *North Star News*, a school newsletter that was designed by students and featured announcements and messages from administration.

North Star News
East Stroudsburg North H.S.
January 2005

TIMBERWOLVES

The monthly newsletter for our High School community!

Snow, ice, or a little of both!

Winter blues getting you down? Well, why don't you consider some community winter family fun at Shawnee Mountain Ski or Fernwood Tubing? Having trouble paying your heating bills? You may qualify for local Heating Assistance Programs by calling the United Way.

National Wear Red Day

On Friday, Feb. 4th please participate to show support for women suffering from heart disease. More women die than men from heart disease (over 40%) and we have to increase that awareness. Please help spread the word. Pins will be on sale for $3.00 to raise money for this very important cause.

Parent Help:

P.S.S.A. 11th Grade Writing test will be administered to all Juniors next month between Feb. 14th-23rd. Parents can support teachers' efforts by reviewing the grading rubric, essay organization, and overall home encouragement. Students perform best when they practice and feel confident that they are well prepared and rested. Other tips for parents and students are available on our website for you. **Guidance Office:** Did you know that our school has a career room? It is adjacent to the guidance office and contains numerous resources for career explorations well as college and financial aid information. There are (10)computers for student use as well as books, catalogs, college applications, and military information. Students in Mrs. Hopstetter's market-

ing class will be working with career counselor, Mrs. Dietz, to market this great resource to all students. Students are welcome during any free period! The career room is also available to any teacher who is interested in bringing their class to meet Mrs. Dietz - (Mrs. Galayda & Mrs. Mathiesen have already taken advantage of this!). Check out additional websites besides our's (www.esasd.net/ehn) such as www . career.missouri.edu, www.collegeboard.com, www.bls.gov and www.pheaamentor.org

BLACK HISTORY MONTH SUGGESTIONS:

If you or someone you know could help the school celebrate Black History Month with an authentic presentation to assist student learning, please contact Ms. Owens in the Main Office to coordinate. Any assistance would be greatly appreciated!!!!

MUSIC DEPARTMENT: A special thank you to Mr. Bakner and Ms. Yosviak and students for their special performance for our School Board this past Jan. 24th. Everyone is very proud of the way you continually demonstrate your talent and dedication to music. Bravo!

Academic Opportunities

Mr.Marcial's World Cultures Class had an exciting culminating event to reinforce the role of the horse throughout history. Students celebrated by saddling up at Milford's Malibu Ranch where they had riding, tacking, and grooming lessons. Mr. Marcial also did a wonderful job assisting new students assimulate to a different world they never had experienced before. Even though many were walking funny the next day, the students had an incredible time and shared their experience through a writing assignment that they presented to their not-so-daring peers.

Mr. Long's Media Production Class: allows students to put on daily news show for announcements. The students learn by doing and have opportunities to anchor, film, edit, and produce building wide newscasts. Students enjoy Mr. Long's expertise while learning the skills of broadcast comm. **Mr. Greene's Woodworking Shop Class** is currently creating furniture. Beginning students are exposed to safety and life skills such as home repair. Special recognition to Brian Dinger for his Ogee Bracket Foot Chest:

An early edition of the school's monthly newsletter.

The students in the music program continued to show excellence and dedication, and having a new amphitheater just down the road from the school, Carty was eager to provide North's singers with new opportunities. Following the success of the 2004 graduation at the Mountain Laurel Center, Richard Bryant told Carty of a composer he knew of who was running songwriting workshops in high schools. The composer's name was Jim Papoulis. "[Bryant] was the one who introduced me to Jim Papoulis and asked if I would be interested in doing something like that. And I said 'Absolutely, yes!'" said Carty. Papoulis, who had only just begun running composer-in-residence programs, was eager to work with the Concert Choir. Papoulis recalls feeling very connected.

"I remember it being a very engaging workshop. The kids were very open, and I was learning how to ask the right questions." According to Papoulis, the first step is establishing a comfortable working environment. He asked them, "what is important to you as a human? For humanity to evolve in a positive way? What makes a good person? And, what is a message you'd like to share with the world?" While sitting at the piano, playing chords, students offered up the hook of what would be a new song.

"If I could live forever, we'd be strong together."

"It's about how we can improve humanity somewhere and we are stronger as a people together than separate. It was a beautiful sentiment from high schoolers," said Papoulis.

Work continued over several weeks, and in the winter of 2005, the song was ready to be recorded. Once again, Carty roused the interest of the nearby Mountain Laurel Center, who allowed the North High School to use its stage for a recording session. "I loved the song they wrote," said Carty. "I was so proud of the talent our students have." Papoulis still recalls the experience at East Stroudsburg North as motivational in his career. "East Stroudsburg was one of the most engaging ones and it really moved me in the direction of working with students. I always try to write music from the vantage point of the person singing it."

Following the success of this experience was the fifth musical, which was *Seussical the Musical*. "Seussical teaches us," wrote Yozviak, "that 'anything's possible,' but a show of this magnitude would definitely NOT be possible without the help and support of many who care." Among the many useful lessons this show imparts on its audience, the simple plea to "tell yourself…how lucky you are" stands out as a nice reminder of the North High School community.

Within two months of the spring musical, a new stadium was finally completed at the football field. Despite the many challenges involved with opening a new school and establishing a new culture, things were progressing nicely.

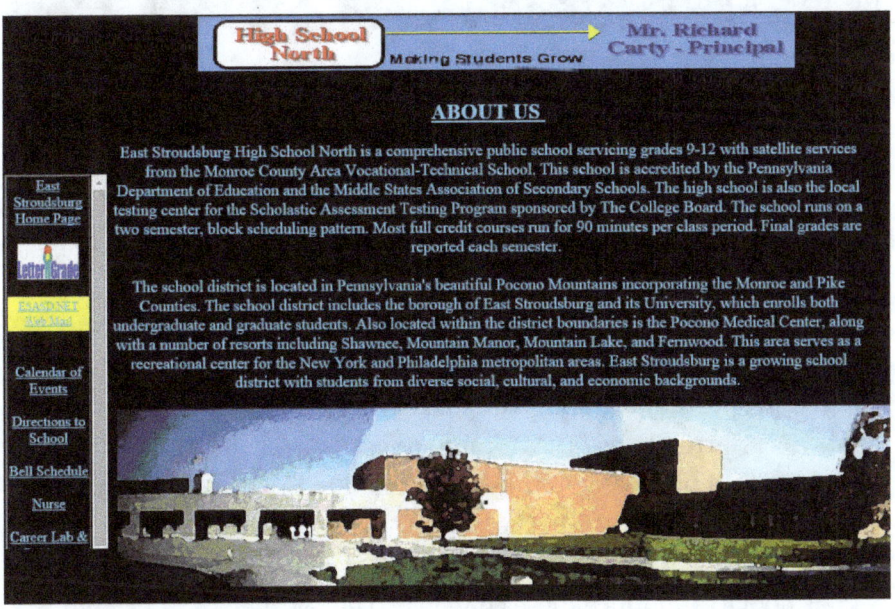

East Stroudsburg Area High School-North

Honors Reception

Honors
2004

May 27, 2004

East Stroudsburg High School North

Seussical

Friday, April 1 7:30 PM
Saturday, April 2 7:30 PM
Sunday, April 3 3:00 PM

Music by STEPHEN FLAHERTY
Lyrics by LYNN AHRENS
Co-Conceived by LYNN AHRENS, STEPHEN
FLAHERT, and ERIC IDLE
Based on the works of DR. SEUSS

LISA YOZVIAK, Director/Musical Director
TODD DEEN, Assistant Musical Director
AJ KISE, Staging/Choreographer
TODD MASON, Choreographer
BOB ROSENBERGER, Drama Coach

Seussical is presented through special arrangement with
Music Theater International
421 West 54th Street New York, NY 10019 www.mtishows.com

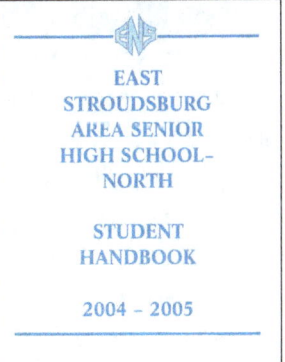

EAST STROUDSBURG AREA SENIOR HIGH SCHOOL-NORTH

STUDENT HANDBOOK

2004 – 2005

The Timberwolves Football Stadium was completed in 2005.

East Stroudsburg North High School had become quite accustomed to change during its first five years. However, none of these changes affected Carty as much as a phone call he received in early April, 2005.

Central Administration was planning a series of administrative changes, largely triggered by the departure of Michael Michaels. This resulted in several building principals being shuffled about as part of what was referred to as "the domino effect." Among these changes, Carty was told that he would be reassigned to Bushkill Elementary School, effective April 15th. Carty was shocked.

During the next week, a faculty meeting was called at the North High School to announce these changes. "The teachers were listening, and nobody said anything," Carty said. "The fear of retribution came when you spoke up." Several teachers, enraged by the decision, flocked to Carty's office to ask him why this had happened. Carty did not know what to say. "In the end, I really didn't have a choice."

Following the April 11, 2005 board meeting where the administrative changes were announced publicly, students became very angry. "When the students and staff found out about it, it was almost a protest!" said Carty. Students made posters, saying "Save Mr. Carty" and "Mr. Carty belongs at ENS," which were hung all over the building. "I got a call from the superintendent. She directed me to have all of the posters removed," said Carty. "I didn't hang them, and I don't know who did, but I said, 'okay,' and they were taken down right away."

Friday, April 15th quickly arrived — Carty's last day at East Stroudsburg North High School. During homeroom, Carty got on the intercom. As part of his farewell, he said, "I really enjoyed my time here, but I won't be that far away. Your new principal is a good person; she will do a great job. Please help make it as smooth of a transition as possible."

After finishing his announcement, Carty heard a knock on his office door. Standing in the hallway was Patricia Mulroy, the former assistant principal, who had been assigned to succeed him as the principal. "She came to me and said, 'you have so much class.' I needed to make this as smooth as possible. I trained her and I considered her to be a friend."

Throughout the day, teachers and students stopped by the office to say goodbye. Carla Mathiesen vividly remembers this.

Julie Tischler and I went into his office, and he's sitting there, trying really hard not to cry, and we were trying really hard not to cry. I looked around the room and I said, 'do you have professional movers coming?' He said, 'no, I'm supposed to do it myself. I just can't. I got the boxes here; I just can't put stuff in them.' I said, 'do you mind if we do it?' 'I'd be honored,' he said. It was hands-down the saddest day of my career.

As students said their goodbyes, Carty said to all the seniors, "I'll see you at graduation." Two months later, when the class of 2005 marched into the Mountain Laurel Center, the processional was led by Carty. He also stood on stage and shook each student's hand just before their name was called.

"That was the most emotional graduation for me," recalls Carty. "A lot of students hugged me, and administration saw."

"Change sometimes is inevitable," said Dailey. "It was a bittersweet kind of thing because everybody loved Mr. Carty.

BUSHKILL ELEMENTARY SCHOOL
HC 12, BOX 700 Dingmans Ferry, PA 18328
Richard Carty, Principal * 570-588-4400 * FAX 570-588-4406 * carty@esasd.net

June 9, 2005

I would like to take this opportunity to thank all of the students, faculty, parents, and family members for all of your support throughout this school year. I would personally like to thank the entire staff of the Mountain Laurel Center for your cooperation in this partnership, and for making this a very special graduation for the students of East Stroudsburg North.

Congratulations to the Class of 2005!

Sincerely,

Richard O. Carty
Principal

Images of Carty at the 2005 graduation and a congratulatory message written by Carty that was printed in the ceremony program.

Seeing him move on was difficult for our staff. But everyone had nothing but respect for Ms. Mulroy." "As a building, we mourned his loss for the rest of that year," said Mathiesen. "Mulroy came in and tried to do what she could do but were all just sad."

Carty recalls this as the most stressful time in his life. "I had no elementary experience, but I took a vow that I would embrace it and prove to the administration that (a) I had more class than that; and (b) I was better than they were."

Third Base
ELEMENTARY SCHOOL

U pon walking into an elementary school, one is often met with a frenzy of organized chaos. Parents escorting their children into the building, staff aides greeting the children, teachers providing directions, musical instruments playing, and walls are decked out in colorful displays. To some, this is a very comfortable and familiar environment. For Richard Carty, it was entirely new.

The announcement of Carty being transferred was a surprise to the Bushkill Elementary School community. Unfortunately, not everyone at Bushkill was happy about the decision. At the April 11, 2005 meeting of the Board of Education, several teachers voiced their dissatisfaction. "I was at this board meeting. A lot of the teachers were not happy about the decision," said Carty. "It's not that they were not happy about *me*."

Since its opening in 1998, Bushkill had seen rapid changes in its administration. The first principal, Eva Haddon, only served for two years. Her successor, Joseph Yanek, served for just over three years. Finally, Patricia Mulroy had just passed the one-year mark as principal by this point. The teachers did not want Mulroy to leave. "They were getting up to the microphone and carrying on something awful," Carty recalls, "and I'm sitting there and I'm thinking to myself, 'what did I get myself into? How am I gonna walk into something like that? They're not happy about having a new person in there, and now I'm gonna go over and move in?'"

After listening to the intensity of the arguments presented by the Bushkill faculty at the meeting, Carty became very uncomfortable. "I was just sitting there like a deer in the headlights! I was thinking, 'this is going to be awful; this is going to be brutal. What did I get myself into?'" Sitting in the meeting room was Jennie Butsch, who was one of the office secretaries at Bushkill. She sensed Carty's discomfort. "She came over, she put her hand on my arm, and she said, "don't worry about a thing, everything is going to be okay, we're gonna take care of you." Carty's long-time colleague Jeffrey Heard remembers offering some encouraging words. "I told him, 'Rico, you're gonna be just as good as you were at the high school. You'll do just as well at the elementary level. The kids will love you; the teachers will appreciate the way you treat them.'"

Bushkill Elementary School

For some of the faculty at Bushkill, Carty's transfer was actually a reacquaintance. Kristen Bueki, who was a 1986 graduate of East Stroudsburg, remembered Carty from her years as a student. "I remember him as a high school teacher, and then he was a high school principal, and now he was an elementary school principal," recalled Bueki. "I was shocked that we were going to work together and that he was now at the elementary level. And, you know what, it turned out to be the best thing ever!"

Moving into a new school very late in the year could disrupt the ebb and flow of the school, but fortunately, faculty members recall it being a very smooth transition. As complimented by Bueki:

He really had the grace to know how to move into this building and so late in the year. April would have been the fourth marking period, three-quarters of the year are gone. And he never once complained. He never once showed he was upset or disgruntled. He never, ever had any negativity. Everything from him was positive and moving in the right direction.

It did not take long for the school community—including faculty, students, and parents— to recognize Carty's character. "We were very glad to have Mr. Carty," said Nadia Worobij, who taught music at Bushkill. "He was the most approachable principal we had. He was very humanistic, he saw the person, what was inside each person whether they were a teacher, a child, or a parent. He really knew how to communicate and he really knew how to listen without judgment." Janine Morley, a member of Bushkill's parent-teacher organization at the time, recalls Carty's introduction. "I remember there was some concern because he was coming down from the upper grades and people wondering 'how is he going to be with the elementary kids,' and everything continued to be fine." "I remember Rico being a little in the dark with the elementary level, but willing to learn," recalled Sandra Borrasso, who taught special education at Bushkill. "He really respected us and respected that we had been there a while." "The children loved him, just like the older kids did," said Heard. "Kids see through things, they know who's being honest and who truly cares, and who's just saying things, and Rico doesn't just say things. Kids see that, they know."

"As the kids got to know him," Bueki remembers, "you would see these tiny little kids—and you can picture Rico, the big, athletic, strapping man that he is—giving hugs and high-fives to these little five-year-olds. It was rather priceless. It was heartwarming."

"He would get out there on the playground with the kids," said Borrasso. "He'd be playing ball with them. He wanted to befriend the kids."

Even in the friendliest of environments, as the principal of a school, one must be ready to deal with disciplinary situations with almost no warning. For Carty, his first disciplinary scenario at the elementary level occurred before he had fully moved into Bushkill Elementary School. "I was watching both buildings," said Carty. "I had not worked there yet but I was on call. I get a phone call from the secretary at Bushkill, saying that two kids pulled the fire alarm."

As soon as the high school's last bus drove away, Carty went over to the elementary school. "I walked into the office and two boys are sitting there. Their feet weren't even touching the floor! I'm thinking, *these* are the guys?" Carty walked over to the secretary, Jan Pelzer, and asked, "Jan, how old are these kids?" Pelzer said, "They're in kindergarten." "Kindergarten! You mean to tell me I have to suspend two kids in kindergarten?" "Yeah, probably," said Pelzer. After speaking with the teacher, Carty brought each child into the office one at a time. "I asked the first kid, 'Why did you do it?' He said, 'Well, I only pulled it *part of* the way! He pulled it the rest of the way!' I couldn't even keep a straight face! And then I asked the second kid the same question, and he responded, 'It said *pull!*' I had to suspend them."

Suspending a student is never an easy process. "It was a big deal. You have to think about all the other kids who were there, they knew what they did was wrong, they knew they weren't supposed to do it, and they did it," said Carty. A few days later, on a Friday afternoon, Pelzer called Carty and said, "A parent dropped off a letter, you're gonna want to see this." Upon entering the Elementary School, Carty opened the letter, and read the first paragraph where he found the passage: *this isn't the high school.* "I knew where this was going," Carty remembered, "I folded it back up, put it in the envelope, and I said [to Pelzer], 'Put it in the drawer, I'll call the parents first thing on Monday morning." Following his own rules, Carty decided not to reply in writing, but instead, got the parents on the phone. "I told them, 'Look, I'm not happy about having to do this either, but whether you're five or fifteen, there has to be consequences for something you have done wrong, and that was the consequence. As much as I hated to do it, I'm pretty sure that they'll never do anything like that again. If there are no consequences, no learning will take place.' And that was the end of that."

Carty tried his best to establish a friendly rapport with his faculty. At the first faculty meeting after his becoming principal at Bushkill, he provided a reminder that every educator needs to hear from time to time. "He told us, 'Remember why you're here: you're here for the child; you're here for the students,'" said Bueki. "'And as long as you keep that as the center of the focus of what you do every day, everything is going to work out fine.'" Borrasso recalls the experience of working with Carty as "more of a conversation. He wasn't authoritative. 'Okay, what do you think works best?' We all appreciated that. We didn't have to make huge transitions when he came to Bushkill."

The success of a school, its culture, and its Parent-Teacher Association is largely reliant on the cooperation of the building's principal, and thankfully, Bushkill's active PTO was able to achieve this very quickly with Carty. "He always seemed really nice and the PTO was very pleased with him," said Morley. "There were no problems with anything that we wanted to do. Any time we had suggestions, I don't remember him having any kind of issue with anything we wanted to do or needed help with." Despite all of the negativity

Richard Carty at Bushkill Elementary

and confusion associated with the transition, Carty had successfully become a receptive and gracious leader in his new building. An unofficial appraisal came early on when a poster was hung outside of the office doorway that read, *Mr. Carty: The Big Man with the Big Heart*. "I remember that poster," said Worobij. "I don't know who put it up there, but it was definitely true. He was generous with his time and an excellent communicator. Ample compassion."

The year 2005 marked both a beginning and a conclusion of a chapter in Carty's life. After three years of studying at Marywood University, while working as a full-time administrator, Carty had finally reached the end of his second Master's degree. In August 2005, Carty received Pennsylvania's Letter of Eligibility to serve as a superintendent, which certified him to work with pre-kindergarten through grade twelve. Carty now had the opportunity to advance to upper-level administration, should he choose to do so. "I thought I wanted to be an assistant superintendent for human resources," said Carty, "but the longer I went, I decided that it's not worth the aggravation. I'm doing just fine [at Bushkill] and I'll stay here until it's time for me to retire, and I'll be fine. And that's just what I did."

As Carty got to know the students at Bushkill, he looked for ways to make their school experience as meaningful and beneficial as possible. One of his earliest initiatives was establishing a Big Brothers-Big Sisters program between Bushkill and the students at the North High School.

Eventually, a school-based mentoring program was established and, in 2006, the school received a $2,500 donation from the Morgan Stanley Volunteer Incentive Program. "We are a school with a strong culture for learning and are dedicated to providing multiple opportunities for our students and school community to become successful learners in and out of the classroom," said Carty in an article by *The Pocono Record*. "Bushkill Elementary mutually benefits with partnerships with home and other members of the community to provide resources, experiences, and interactions for students and staff." The launch of this program was more than an administrative project for Carty, as it was an effort he was once a part of. "A donation like this is close to my heart...I was a volunteer with Big Brothers-Big Sisters throughout my four years of college. This truly is a great organization whose main goals are to recreate the extended family through friendship, guidance, and love."

As a high school principal, Carty sought to include students in decision making and provided them with a voice. Upon moving to the elementary school, he continued this belief by encouraging students to develop conduct rules for the school.

Carty appears on "North News" in 2005 to invite North High School students to participate in Big Brothers-Big Sisters

The result of this effort was "The Timberwolf Ts:"

Take responsibility, Try your best, and Treat others with respect.

"I always follow the KISS method: Keep It Simple, Stupid," said Carty. "It's not rocket science! If you do something wrong, it's your fault, but if you do something right, it's your fault, too." More than simply teaching rules, Carty wanted to ensure that disciplinary infractions were not repeated. "My biggest fear was a student coming back to my office the next day, or the next week, or two weeks later for doing the same thing, because then I'm worried that they haven't learned from this."

Carty did his best to instill a sense of pride in the school among the student body, hoping to incentivize good behavior. "Take pride in your pack" was echoed throughout the building. Carty also made it a priority to address bullying, which is an ongoing problem in many schools. In December of 2007, a school-wide pledge was signed by every student, certifying Bushkill Elementary School as a "No Place for Hate School." According to the meeting minutes, students promised "to combat intolerance, bullying and hatred in our school." Throughout the remainder of the year, numerous activities were planned that "celebrate diversity and promote respect for differences."

While helping students develop socially and emotionally was important, Carty wanted to provide engaging learning opportunities.

One opportunity presented itself when Carty learned of the opening of a new non-profit organization called Junior Achievement, based in Luzerne County. This organization, as described in a *Pocono Record* article, "uses hands-on educational programs to prepare students for the global marketplace." In collaboration with fifth-grade teacher Elyse Vitchers, Carty organized a field trip for the fifth-grade class to "JA BizTown," which was a replica of a small town. Students assumed the roles of business owners and consumers, learning practical lessons in money management and economics. When interviewed in 2007, Carty stated that "I thought [this program] would help and be a great experience for the kids. Lots of times it's harder to make real-life connections for kids in elementary school than it is in high school." In the 2008 yearbook, Carty acknowledged this event in his message to the student body:

> I am extremely proud of our fifth grade class for their hard work, effort, and performance that they demonstrated at JA BizTown. You have left me with many positive memories, and have established a benchmark for future classes to work.

The academic performance of a school is an ongoing concern of any school principal, and Carty was no exception to this. At the time, Bushkill Elementary School was not performing at a desirable standard in reading and mathematics. "We were having issues with test scores," Carty recalls. "We had a very high population of economically disadvantaged students." Curious to know how other schools addressed such a population, Carty called an elementary school in the Easton School District that seemed to have a similar population to that of Bushkill. "When I called there, they had an assistant principal. They had less kids than we did, and I did not have an assistant principal." At the time, Bushkill had a student population of about 560 students, which is large for an elementary school. "My question to them was, 'How many reading teachers do you have?' She said, 'We have four reading teachers and four instructional aides.' We [at Bushkill] had two reading teachers and two instructional aides." Carty thought to himself, "How can we possibly get this done when we don't have enough staff to get these kids to where they need to be?" Unfortunately, despite Bushkill having the lowest test scores in the district, Carty's request to hire an additional reading teacher and an instructional aide was not approved. "I wanted to say, 'Don't stand there and trash us because our students did not pass these tests when we don't have enough resources to improve what we need to improve!'" Carty knew that he would need to find creative ways to boost academic performance with the limited resources given to him.

In 2008, the topic of full-day kindergarten appeared on the board meeting's agenda. Thanks to grant funding, each elementary school in the district had one full-day kindergarten class in addition to several half-day sections. To many people's surprise, full-day kindergarten was no longer deemed financially feasible. Fearing the negative effects of losing this critical instruction time, Carty requested to make a presentation at the next Board meeting. "I told them that sixty percent of our students had failed kindergarten screening. Basically, sixty percent of our students were not ready for kindergarten. We've closed the gap considerably, but we did not close it completely because they were so far behind when they got here. If you take away full-day kindergarten, we are going in reverse order." Carty was deeply concerned for his students. "We had kids coming in who didn't know their colors, their letters...they couldn't write their name. These are very basic things. We had sixty percent of our kids who couldn't do those things." In late 2009, the Board of Education moved to place Bushkill Elementary School on a School Improvement Plan.

Change needed to occur, and it needed to occur quickly. Bushkill was a crowded building and lacked the personnel needed to make the changes required by the state. Carty decided that partnerships with supplemental education services could be a step in the right direction, and in 2010, Bushkill partnered with six different providers. These included Learner First, Sylvan Learning Center of Monroe and Pike Counties, and The Learning Lamp, among others. Carty was curious to see how neighboring school districts addressed similar challenges. Delaware Valley School District, located less than thirty miles north, was performing at a much higher rate than East Stroudsburg. Carty looked at their programs and discovered one in particular that could help his students. "I started another program funded by the state, a Pre-K program," said Carty. "Unfortunately, it was only half a day. We only had ten kids in the morning session and ten kids in the afternoon session, but the way I looked at it, that was twenty more kids well prepared for kindergarten." Carty took several teachers from Bushkill up to Delaware Valley to learn about their program. "Not every elementary school in our district did that, but we did because I said we need it. As a teacher, you can't sit there and blame the parents. We have to try anything and everything to get the students to where they need to be. We need every resource in our power early to get them squared away."

These efforts proved successful. In September 2010, Bushkill Elementary School saw progress in all of the required areas of the improvement plan except for reading among students with individualized evaluation plans. Of the twenty-five "adequate yearly progress targets," Bushkill met twenty-four of them. This was laudable, but work still needed to be done. Bushkill Elementary School was now placed on "School Improvement 2," a continuation of the original school improvement plan.

Carty looked closely at the amount of time provided for students to work on their math and reading skills. Working with his faculty, Carty devised a new schedule that loosely resembled the intensive scheduling format used in the high schools. The new schedule provided for ninety minutes of uninterrupted reading instruction, followed by a daily enrichment and intervention period. Furthermore, sixty minutes of mathematics instruction was allocated, with daily math review sessions integrated into homeroom time. Recognizing the validity of Carty's findings, in 2010, the district hired an additional reading instructional aide for Bushkill. By doing this, it provided "additional students the opportunity for small group intervention...and enables homeroom teachers more opportunity to work with students to help maintain and enrich grade level skills." Carty also sought the expertise of the Step by Step Learning consulting firm to provide professional development opportunities in reading instruction for the faculty. Everyone in the building, from faculty to students, realized the importance of this effort.

The 2010–11 school year also marked the beginning of a School-Wide Positive Behavior Support program, as Carty realized that academic performance and behavior are closely correlated. Remembering his coaching philosophy of "spelling out the expectations," Carty and his faculty defined all of the expected student behaviors and developed lesson plans for teaching these behaviors. Attempting to keep the morale high, a "kick-off assembly" was held in the form of a pep rally. In attendance were athletes and cheerleaders from the North High School, accompanied by the Timberwolf mascot. As a bonus, through this experience, students learned how to behave during an assembly. The program was successful in its first year and proved successful for several years into the future.

Academic progress continued in a positive direction. By mid-2011, district administrators were visiting other school districts to seek advice and examples to follow. Bushkill Elementary School continued to employ the services of external providers for supplemental education services. In particular, the contract with Step by Step Learning was proving very successful. At the July 18, 2011 meeting of the Board of Education, Mr. Carty addressed the progress made in his building. Most notably, he noted that students began the 2010–11 school year with a 29% benchmark and are now at a 73% benchmark. As published in the Board meeting minutes, "Mr. Carty stated that he believes the kids made incredible gains which are attributed to the work we are doing with Step by Step because prior, we were not getting there." Everyone's hard work had paid off.

Despite the often-stressful nature of remedial education, the students at Bushkill Elementary School received an enriching, positive experience at school. "Things really flourished under Mr. Carty," said Worobij. "We had lots of musicals every year, the parents became involved, they made the scenery for our productions. The parents were really involved during Mr. Carty's time. And the teachers wanted to do stuff. They sang during our holiday programs. He encouraged that. We had different directors come in; he allowed us to set that up. He came to all of our concerts, he was there all the time, and supporting us all the time. That means a lot to teachers."

Another yearly event to take place during Carty's tenure at
Bushkill was a Science and Art Fair. "The students had to create a
project using the scientific method in their investigation," explained
Jennifer Peruso, who taught fourth grade and organized the fair. "The
projects were created at home and parents provided the supplies.
The goal was for the students to pose a scientific question and then
use the scientific method in their investigation to come up with an
answer to that question." Additionally, an annual event was created
to incentivize reading instruction. "Family reading night was pretty
well-attended," said Borrasso. "

As time went on, families got much more involved with their kids."

Other initiatives were developed to build positive feelings about reading and language arts, such as "Spring into Reading" and participation in the Elks Essay Contest, sponsored by the East Stroudsburg Elks Lodge. Patriotism was celebrated through events like a school-wide Veterans Day Walk across the North campus.

All the while, fourth and fifth grades could participate in a wide variety of after-school activities, ranging from African Drumming to the Young Author's Club. Finally, Bushkill continued to educate fifth graders on the dangers of drugs through the D.A.R.E. (Drug Abuse Resistance Education) program, led by Sheriff Phil Bueki. By 2012, Bushkill was the only school in the East Stroudsburg Area School District and one of the only schools in Pike County that still offered the D.A.R.E. program. "We are so lucky to still be able to fund this program," said Carty in an interview for *The Pocono Record*. "These kids are very lucky to have Sheriff Bueki, their parents, Lehman Township Board and taxpayers to support this much needed and worthy program."

Fifth graders graduate from the D.A.R.E Program.

School days for "the Timbercubs," as they were so affectionally named, were full of positive, meaningful learning experiences that kept true to the school's mission to serve as "a culturally diverse, rapidly growing, united community, [creating] a solid foundation in shaping each student to become a positive, respectful, well-rounded citizen on a lifelong journey of success."

Having worked at the high school level for so many years, Carty witnessed many students reach adulthood, which is gratifying for any educator. But now he got to witness a more precious period of youth, which he reflected on in his 2011 yearbook message: "To the 5th grade class: I have known many of you since kindergarten, and it's been exciting to watch you grow up. I wish you the very best and continued success throughout your educational careers."

Clockwise: Veterans Walk; Planting a tree in a student's memory; 2012 winners of the Elks Essay Contest.

By the time he reached his seventh year as principal, Carty had seen tremendous changes at Bushkill. The Internet had become a crucial component of many of the day-to-day tasks of running a school. The emphasis on standardized test preparation shaped much of the instructional processes being carried out in the classrooms. Many of Carty's initiatives were successful. The School-Wide Positive Behavior Support Program was exceeding expectations. Most notably, Bushkill finally met all twenty-five of the Annual Yearly Progress

Goals and was on its way to no longer needing a school improvement plan. Carty now felt the time had come to retire, and in March of 2012, he announced his intent to retire that summer.

1. **Retirement**	
Name	**Position Held**
a. Carty, Richard	Principal - Bushkill Elementary Effective Date: at the end of the workday on July 6, 2012.

Minutes of the March 19, 2012 school board meeting, announcing Carty's retirement.

"I didn't want anyone to know but, in our district, you had to submit your notice three months in advance. That was a rule," said Carty. "The reason I didn't want anybody to know that is because whenever people find out someone is retiring, they think 'He doesn't care anymore, he's just going through the motions.' I made a vow that I was not going to overlook anything or push anything aside. I was going to continue to do whatever I did until the last day I walked out of there."

Faculty members recall Carty's final year as emotional. "We knew it was the end of an era and we knew that we were blessed for those seven years," said Bueki. "And his work ethic was the same: he worked as hard the day he left as the day he came. He was always present, he was always hands-on, right up to the end." In his message to the students in the 2012 yearbook, Carty chose not to emphasize his departure but instead provided a simple, positive message.

It has been a pleasure to work with all of the students at BES and watch you grow academically and mature as students. I wish each and every student a safe and happy summer vacation.
Fifth graders: as you move on to Lehman Intermediate and High School North, I wish you continued success.
Make us Timberwolf proud!

A proper send-off was in order. One of Carty's least favorite tasks was reviewing tapes from the cameras on school buses. "In elementary school, you always had issues on the buses," said Carty. "I spent a lot of time looking at tapes and watching kids shove another kid into the ground, and then we had to throw somebody off the bus, call their parents, and it was tiring. If you had to go through a bus tape and investigate something, you were looking at a couple of hours." This undesirable activity provided inspiration to the faculty. "It's the last day of school and I'm in my office," Carty recalls. "On the last day, there's a lot of stuff going on, and I'm trying to wrap things up." As Carty was working, a guidance counselor entered his office in a hurry. "A bus driver just dropped off a bus videotape. You need to see this." Carty, surprised, responded, "You've gotta be kidding me! It's the last day! I don't have time for that." He asks the guidance counselor to roll the TV out of his office and watch the videotape for him. About ten to fifteen minutes later, she returned to Carty's office and said, "You're gonna want to see this." "Where's the TV?" asked Carty. "I took it down to the library," said the counselor.

As Carty walked to the library, he thought to himself, "It's the last day of school, how could this be?" Carty entered the library where he found many of the teachers. The guidance counselor puts the tape into the VCR and hits the play button, and Carty could not have anticipated what he was about to see.

> After the last bus dropped off the kids, the bus came back to Bushkill and all the teachers got on the bus. And they were carrying on, they had their arms out the window, they had their heads out the window, hollering, throwing paper balls and stuff around, and then each one of them got up and walked toward the camera and, one by one, each teacher looked at the camera and said something about me until each teacher got off the bus.

"It was pretty funny! They knew how tortured I was watching bus tapes," said Carty. "We really, really, really missed him after he left," said Worobij. "Rico had the most impact in my life as a principal and as a person."

On July 6, 2012, on a Friday afternoon, Carty walked out the front doors of Bushkill Elementary School for the last time, leaving thirty-one years with the East Stroudsburg Area School District behind him. "The last day I walked out of there…it was the weirdest feeling in the world. It was so hard to believe it was over. It was weird, it really was." The faculty and staff at Bushkill threw a retirement party for Carty at Pub 209, which Carty still recalls as very special night.

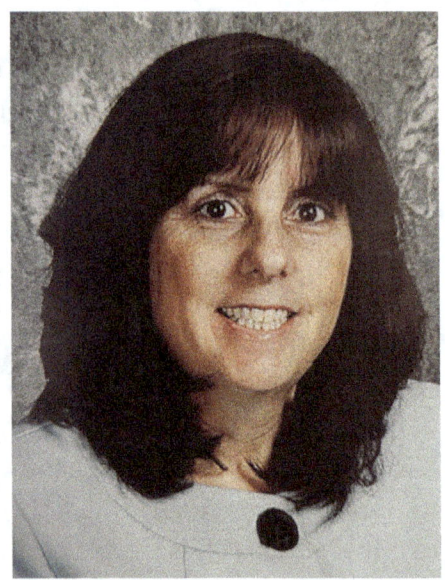

Richard Carty's 2012 yearbook photo; Debra Padavano

Following Carty's retirement, former colleague Debra Padavano transferred to Bushkill from the North High School. Similarly, to Carty, Padavano was new to working in an elementary school setting. "I was in the high school for sixteen years and now, all of the sudden, I was in elementary land," recalls Padavano. "It was a whole different world! Thankfully, the staff was very good and helped me out and showed me the way." Padavano soon realized the impact Carty had made over his seven years at Bushkill as well as the team spirit in the building. "Bushkill has one of the closest staffs. Their staff is very much aligned with one another. They help each other out. They all loved Mr. Carty there. The kids and the staff."

Home Run
EPILOGUE

After turning left onto Bushkill Falls Road, the 6.3-mile drive to East Stroudsburg's North Campus is similar today to the way it was in 2000, yet somewhat unrecognizable.

The roadway is wider, and business signage has changed, but the natural beauty of the forest continues to provide an unobtrusive backdrop. One can still turn left and find Bushkill Elementary School which continues to make positive strides under Matt Sadowsky's leadership. The East Stroudsburg North High School has come into its own over the past two decades, seeing increased school spirit, parental involvement, and excellence throughout the subject areas. The building's fourth principal, Benjamin Brenneman, has guided the school through periods of rapid technological advancements, facility upgrades, and the unprecedented Coronavirus Pandemic. The spirit of open-minded resilience that was present when the building opened is still stronger than ever.

Following his retirement in 2012, Richard Carty stayed connected to the schools he oversaw. He proudly attended Spring into Reading at Bushkill for many years and continued to enjoy watching the Timberwolf sports teams compete.

In 2014, two years after his retirement, Carty was bestowed one of East Stroudsburg's highest honors when he was inducted into the Athletic Hall of Fame. This honor, as described on the district's website, "was instituted in 2002 to honor those who have brought honor and prestige to the East Stroudsburg Area School District and its community." He was nominated by former assistant baseball coach and longtime friend Jeffrey Heard. "He enjoyed being with those kids and athletes, helping them not only become better athletes but better people. He took a lot of pride in that," said Jeff Heard. "He deserved it," said Douglas Arnold, who coached football with Carty. "We don't have a lot of baseball championships, but he won one. There's not a whole lot of multi-sport championship head coaches either."

It was during Carty's years as principal of East Stroudsburg High School North when the Hall of Fame was established. Every other year, the induction ceremony is held at the North Campus. "Some of the great speeches by recipients were from North people," said Arnold. "It kinda moved people to know that this new school had turned out such tremendous new people. Whether they were musicians or athletes or people who did great things in the community. And the North community is always so welcoming, they do a wonderful job when we go up there." As the principal at the time, Carty wanted the honorees and their families to be treated gracefully in his building, but at the time, he never thought that he would later be nominated.

On February 7, 2014, the cafeteria at East Stroudsburg High School South was filled with alumni, former coaches, and their loved ones. Carty, who was one of four being honored that night, was surprised when he discovered that one of the other inductees was a graduate of the North High School. Everett Alers, who graduated in 2003, played football and basketball during the first three years of the North High School's history. Carty immediately remembered the first encounter he had with Alers and his mother, fourteen years prior. The audience took their seats and Mark Brown, former coach, athletic director, and friend of Carty, welcomed everyone. Upon calling Carty to the stage, the room filled with applause. "I just remember thanking people that helped me along the way and talking about how I got to where I was," Carty recalled.

"I thanked every kid who ever played for me because, without them, I'm not standing here today."

While at the microphone, Carty looked over to Alers, and then looked out into the audience and saw his mother there.

> Everett was one of those kids who you never saw outside of his element. I remember when Everett's mother brought them into the North High School for the first time. She was a nervous wreck, she was so worried about her boys, and I could see the worry in her eyes. I remember saying to her, 'Ma'am, don't worry about a thing, we'll take good care of your boys.' But you'll be proud to know that your boys took care of themselves. I loved watching Everett compete, he was such a good athlete, he was a good person, and I'm so proud of him.

After the speeches concluded, people came up to Carty. "That means a lot to a parent. She also remembered that first day. People came up afterward and thought that it was unbelievable that I included that in *my* night. He meant as much to me as it meant for me to be inducted." In the years that followed, Carty became a member of the Hall of Fame Committee and, as of this writing, continues to volunteer in this role.

Carty's Hall of Fame plaque on the wall at East Stroudsburg North High School

Through the course of a career in education, one encounters many students and oftentimes wonders what happened to them as the years march onward. "You don't know what kind of job you're doing until these kids are out of school for ten years," said Carty. One day, Carty went to a local pharmacy. Upon walking into the store, he heard someone call his name. Carty looked over and saw a student who had frequently been on the discipline list while in high school. "He was so proud of himself that he had a job," said Carty. "He was a handful, but I never made it personal. I had to suspend this kid so many times, but the way I did it, he'd look at me and say, 'Okay, Mr. Carty, I'll see you in three days.'"

Carty stopped to chat with this former student and acknowledged that the student always accepted his punishment the way he should have. "The last time I had to deal with him, he had called a female teacher the 'c-word.' I remember looking at the write-up and shaking my head. 'Did you really say this?' I asked him. He looked at me and nodded his head. 'I can't believe you'd talk to someone like that. You don't talk to me like that!'"

The student responded in a way Carty will never forget.

"You're different."

"What do you mean?" asked Carty.

"You listen to me," said the student.

Carty realized just how valuable that can be for a student, especially when there was a definite personal dislike toward this student among the faculty. "I let him tell his side of the story; I listened to him. I always focused on what a student did, right or wrong, and I never made it personal." Carty walked through the pharmacy realizing that his strategy had worked, and, despite the frequent disciplinary infractions that this student accrued in high school, Carty was very happy to catch up with him.

When asking someone about their memories of their high school principal, responses often range from remembering an enigmatic presence to suppressed frustration. Many of the students who attended East Stroudsburg High School North during the first five years have a more positive recollection of Carty.

As Randy Paolino, who was part of the first graduating class, recalls:

> The principal is always an intimidating role to the students,
> the whole cliché of 'you're gonna get sent to the principal's office.'
> I don't remember him having that mystique about him at all. That
> might have been my own personal relationship with him, but I
> don't remember him being an intimidating principal or anyone
> who was afraid of him. I have memories of him walking around
> in the halls in between classes with a big smile on his face. He was
> a jovial guy, interactive with students in a positive way. And from
> the group of friends I had, I think that was their perspective as
> well. He was just a cool guy, a nice guy. I remember a strong
> element of school spirit and he really was one of the driving forces
> behind that. Getting excitement in students minds and being
> prideful for being at this new school and making it our own.

A building principal is not only an administrator who deals with
students, parents, and school programs, but they are also a manager.
To the teachers in a particular school, the principal is their boss, and
the impression they get from their principal sets the tone for morale at
work. "He honestly was a big reason why many of us went up to the
North High School," said Darrin Dobrowolski. "His office was always
open, you could always go in and chit-chat with him, he had a good
rapport with the staff and the students." "He is someone as a young
teacher that you wanted to work for," said Ryan Frable. "He made
you feel very comfortable."

Jim Reynolds, who originally hired Carty to coach, offers positive
feedback on his career.

> He really developed a lot of good relationships. The kids loved
> him. He could work them hard and instead of going off the field
> grumbling and complaining, they loved him. And I think the
> students up at the North School did too. He had a great rapport
> with the parents up there. He's just a down to earth guy. He
> doesn't take a lot of crap from anybody but he's a down to earth
> guy. He would listen to people and make his decisions accordingly.

Richard Carty's career is an excellent example of how valuable interpersonal communication is toward the success of a school, a team, or a company. Seeking input from everybody, listening, even if you disagree, making expectations clear, and keeping things simple were some of Carty's professional credos and some of the traits that garnered him respect and appreciation.

In an age where many "leaders" use their email accounts as their main point of contact with their colleagues, it is important to consider the value of authentic communication. Taking the time to speak to others and assure them that they were listened to is vital in earning trust. Carty welcomed his staff and students to speak with him, wanting to get to know them as people and help them to be their best. Nadia Worobij recalls an instance of this. "He asked me, 'How do you want to be remembered later in life?' He really made me evaluate myself and he did it in a very humble, humanistic way. It really helped me change as a person for the better, and I have him to thank for that. He was genuinely interested in my progress as a human being, not only as a teacher, and wanted me to always be my best."

Furthermore, it is a reminder that we must not let ego or differences in personality make professional differences personal. As a school principal, and a manager of employees, Carty always strived to "discipline with dignity," reminding them that a rule may have been broken, and consequences may need to be imposed, but it is not personal. "Being a change agent is the hardest part," says Carty, "but people will have more respect if they think they've been listened to." Such a simple statement, yet, so many people in leadership roles often overlook it. Fortunately, East Stroudsburg High School North's first principal achieved a positive rapport in his building which is remembered and appreciated nearly a quarter of a century later.

Following the tenth anniversary of the opening of East Stroudsburg's North Campus, I had decided to create an oral history series as a gift to my alma mater. I realized that so much had changed in a short amount of time and I wanted to help preserve the school's young history. In January 2012, almost five years after graduating from the

North High School, I drove up to Bushkill Elementary School to interview Carty. On that snowy Thursday afternoon, I walked into Carty's office with a borrowed video camera and we recorded a forty-five-minute interview. Little did I know at the time that he would be retiring later that year. Over the next few years, I made little progress on the oral history project as college, work, and other obligations kept getting in the way.

In the summer of 2020, I realized that the twentieth anniversary of the school's opening was approaching. Due to the Coronavirus Pandemic, I knew that I would not be able to visit the building or plan anything to mark the occasion. By that point, I had not made much progress on the oral history project, and this was not the time to request interviews.

So, I decided to send cards to some of my teachers who had taught at the North High School since opening day. I searched and found an address for Carty, not completely sure if it was accurate, and I wrote him a short letter. A few days later, I got a phone call from an unfamiliar number, only to discover it was Mr. Carty. I had not spoken to him since 2012, eight years prior when I interviewed him. He sounded exactly the same as I remembered.

As the pandemic restrictions were lifted and life returned to normal, I made it a priority to continue the oral history project. To date, over forty hours of interviews have been recorded. A common theme I heard throughout my conversations with faculty, staff, and alumni was the positive memories they had about Carty as their principal. I said to myself, "Other people need to hear these stories. People could really learn something. I should compile these."

And that is what you've just read.

To bring this story to a close, I will offer the closing question I asked everyone I interviewed in the series: *if you had one piece of advice that you could leave to any high school senior who is about to graduate, what would it be?* Carty's response:

Be a good person, treat others like you'd like to be treated, believe in yourself, and remember that you can do anything you desire as long as you're willing to pay the price. And don't let anybody tell you that you can't do something.

Exactly twelve years after Carty spoke on tape, I met him for lunch in East Stroudsburg. After finishing our meals, Carty offered up a nice reflection on his career:

Was I the smartest guy in the world? Probably not. But I had good common sense and I had a good feel for people. And I had a good feel for students. I wanted everyone to feel that they belonged, that they were important, and that they mattered.
That they meant something.

Let us commend Richard Carty for an impressive career, a job well done as a principal, coach, mentor, and role model. May God grant him and his wife many happy years together.

REFERENCES

Documents and Reports

East Stroudsburg Area School District (2014). Athletic Hall of Fame Press Release. https://www.esasd.net/site/handlers/filedownload.ashx?moduleinstanceid=2991&dataid=3550&FileName=Athletic%20Hall%20of%20Fame%20Press%20Release%202014.pdf

East Stroudsburg Area Senior High School North (2001). Student Schedule 2000-2001. [Computer printout].

ESASD (2012, May 21). Meeting Minutes.

ESASD (2012, March 19). Meeting Minutes, p. 11

ESASD (2010, Dec. 20). Meeting Minutes.

ESASD (2009, Nov. 16). Meeting Minutes.

ESASD (2005, Sept. 19). Meeting Minutes.

ESASD (2005, April 11). Meeting Minutes.

ESASD (1999, Dec. 20). Meeting Minutes, pp. 52-53.

ESASD (1999, Sept. 27). Meeting Minutes, p. 13.

ESASD (1998, Nov. 16). Meeting Minutes, p. 261.

ESASD (1997, Nov. 17). Meeting Minutes, p. 125.

ESASD (1995, July 17). Meeting Minutes, p. 204.

ESASD (1995, June 26). Meeting Minutes, p. 119.

ESASD (1995, March 20). Meeting Minutes, p. 49.

ESASD (1995, Feb. 23). Meeting Minutes, p. 27.

ESASD (1995, Jan. 23). Meeting Minutes, p. 2

ESASD (1994, Jan. 18). Meeting Minutes, page unknown.

ESASD (1993, Nov. 18). Meeting minutes, page unknown.

ESASD (1993, August 16). Meeting Minutes, p. 418.

ESASD (1992, May 18). Meeting Minutes, pp. 67, 70.

ESASD (1992, Feb. 17). Meeting Minutes, p. 19.

ESASD (1989, Nov. 28). Meeting Minutes, p. 117.

ESASD (1989, Sept. 18). Meeting Minutes, p. 96.

ESASD (1988, March 21). Meeting Minutes, p. 158.

ESASD (1987, Sept. 21). Meeting Minutes, p. 91.

ESASD (1987, June 22). Meeting Minutes, p. 46.

ESASD (1982, August 16). Meeting Minutes, page unknown.

ESASD (1981, March 21). Meeting Minutes, p. 73.

Greenwood, P. W., & Turner, S. (1987, Nov.). *The VisionQuest Program: An Evaluation*. RAND Corporation.

Files

Carty, R. O. (2000). "East Stroudsburg Area Senior High School North Mission Statement". East Stroudsburg Area School District.

Carty, R. O. (2000). "East Stroudsburg Area Senior High School North Philosophy." East Stroudsburg Area School District.

Haddon, E. W. (1998). "Bushkill Elementary School Mission Statement." East Stroudsburg Area School District.

Institutional Publications

East Stroudsburg Area Senior High School. (2000). *Commencement Program 2000*.

East Stroudsburg Area Senior High School. (1999). *East Stroudsburg High Schools North/South Campus: Program of Studies 2000–2001*.

East Stroudsburg Area Senior High School North. (2005). *Commencement Program 2005*.

East Stroudsburg Area Senior High School North. (2005). *North Star News*, January 2005.

East Stroudsburg Area Senior High School North. (2004). *Student Handbook 2004–2005*.

East Stroudsburg Area Senior High School North. (2004). *Honors Reception Program 2004*.

East Stroudsburg Area Senior High School North. (2004). *Commencement Program 2004*.

East Stroudsburg Area Senior High School North. (2004). *The Wizard of Oz Program*.

East Stroudsburg Area Senior High School North. (2003). *The Wolf Pack Chronicle*, 1(1). [Cover page scan].

East Stroudsburg Area Senior High School North. (2003). *Program of Studies 2003 through 2005*.

East Stroudsburg Area Senior High School North. (2003). *Chicago Program.*

East Stroudsburg Area Senior High School North. (2002). *Footloose Program.*

East Stroudsburg Area Senior High School North. (2001). *Football Game Day Program,* Fall 2001 Season.

East Stroudsburg Area Senior High School North. (2001). *First Annual Spring Concert Program 2001.*

East Stroudsburg Area Senior High School North. (2001). *Timberwolves Chronicle, 1*(5). Senior Issue.

East Stroudsburg Area Senior High School North. (2001). *Godspell Program.*

East Stroudsburg Area Senior High School North. (2000). *Fall Sports Schedule 2000–2001.*

East Stroudsburg Area Senior High School North. (2000). *Football Game Day Program,* Fall 2000 Season.

East Stroudsburg Area Senior High School North. (2000). *Student-Parent Handbook 2000–2001.*

East Stroudsburg Area Senior High School North. (2000). *Winter Concert Program 2000.*

East Stroudsburg Area Senior High School North. (2000). *Timberwolves Chronicle, 1*(1). [Cover page scan].

East Stroudsburg Area School District. (2000). *Dedication Ceremony Program.*

East Stroudsburg University. (1992). *Graduate Catalog.*

East Stroudsburg University. (1990). *Commencement Program 1990.*

Mansfield State College. (1978). *Commencement Program 1978.*

Mansfield State College. (1974). *College Catalog 1974–75.*

Interviews

Anderson, Eric. March 15, 2022.

Anderson, MaryGrace. March 15, 2022.

Arnold, Douglas. July 12, 2022.

Bakner, Paul. February 8, 2022.

Berke, Bruce. March 25, 2022.

Borrasso, Sandra. January 13, 2023.

Brown, Mark. June 23, 2022.

Bueki, Kristen. February 23, 2022.

Carty, Richard. July 1, 2024.

Carty, Richard. January 12, 2024.

Carty, Richard. October 6, 2023.

Carty, Richard. July 21, 2023.

Carty, Richard. February 24, 2023.

Carty, Richard. January 12, 2012.

Dailey, Charles. August 22, 2022.

David, P. William. March 31, 2022.

Dobrowolski, Darrin. March 12, 2022.

Doyle, John. October 23, 2022.

Edwards, Sean. March 28, 2022.

Forsyth, Eric. June 20, 2024.

Frable, Ryan. March 23, 2022.

Green, Robert. January 13, 2023.

Green, Robert. April 7, 2022.

Harris, Tim. January 13, 2023.

Heard, Jeffrey. February 26, 2022.

Johnson, Frank. July 6, 2022.

Kish, Jason. February 10, 2022.

Krupski, Diane. October 20, 2024.

Leibig, Trish. November 28, 2022.

Lewis, Kelly. February 24, 2023.

Lombardo, Angeline. March 25, 2022.

Long, Craig. August 13, 2019.

Marcial, Lawrence. March 4, 2022.

Mathiesen, Carla. February 1, 2022.

McGovern, James. July 24, 2019.

Mochan, Karen. September 28, 2022.

Morley, Janine. August 5, 2022.

Mulroy, Patricia. February 20, 2023.

Nace, Kevin. December 2, 2022.

Nace, Kevin. March 30, 2022.

Padavano, Debra. August 9, 2022.

Paolino, Randy. January 5, 2023.

Papoulis, Jim. July 9, 2024.

Pawlikowski, Bradley. February 7, 2022.

Rambone, Kelly. August 18, 2022.

Reynolds, Jim. July 7, 2022.

Roberts, Tamika. March 27, 2023.

Sherman, Melissa. February 7, 2022.

Soskil, Lori. April 1, 2022.

Tischler, Julie. April 8, 2022.

Voglino, Kevin. January 30, 2022.

Wilson, Susan. May 13, 2022.

Worobij, Nadia. October 8, 2023.

Zasada, Edward. July 5, 2022.

Motion Media

Aslan, V. (2005). The Fifth Commencement: East Stroudsburg Area Senior High School North. [Still frames from DVD].

Aslan, V. (2004). The Fourth Commencement: East Stroudsburg Area Senior High School North. [Still frame from DVD].

North News. (2005). Big Brothers-Big Sisters Program Announcement. [Still frame from videotape].

North News. (2003). Fall 2003 Introduction Montage. [Still frame from videotape].

North News. (2002). Spring 2002 Introduction Title. [Still frame from videotape].

Musical Compositions

Albrecht, S. K. (nd). "For Just a Little While." MMI by Alfred Publishing.

Butler, W. G. (1917). "Mansfield, Hail." [Alma Mater of Mansfield State College].

Contorno, C., Gentile, L., Gioia, D., Gioia, N., McCalla, L., McCarron, R., Samonte, M., Warmbir, L., & Wertz. D. (2000). "East Stroudsburg Area North Alma Mater." [Alma Mater of East Stroudsburg Area Senior High School North].

Papoulis, J., Bombieri, C., Raum, S., & the East Stroudsburg Area
Senior High School North Concert Choir. (2005). "If I Could."
[Original composition and recording developed during a
composer-in-residence workshop].

Porterfield, S. (2000). "Voice of a New Beginning." Heritage
Music Press.

Slider, M. (1931). "The Purple and the White." [Alma Mater of
East Stroudsburg Area Senior High School South].

Newspaper Articles

Applegate, A. (2004, May 29). Mtn. Laurel eyed for grad ceremony.
Pocono Record.

Berrett, D. (2007, Nov. 21). "Children in charge at life-size replica of
American town." *Pocono Record.*

Blockus, G. R. (1988, May 14). "Notre Dame clinches 2A playoff spot."
The Morning Call.

Carey, S. (2007, April 7). "Grant funds Bushkill mentoring program."
Pocono Record.

Connolly, S. (1989, August 21). "E. Stroudsburg construction won't
delay school." *The Morning Call.*

Eldridge, M. (2002, June 6). "Eastburg North graduates first class."
Pocono Record.

Garcia, V. (2000, Nov. 20). "Step Team: A 'new wave' in School Spirit." *Timberwolves Chronicle.*

Lynch, F. (2003, Oct. 31). "New Asst. Principal finds diversity a plus."
The Wolf Pack Chronicle.

Meixell, T. (1989, June 1). "Reenock's arm, bat lift kids past E. Stroudsburg." *The Morning Call.*

Meixell, T. (1989, May 27). "East Stroudsburg whips Dieruff 13-6).
The Morning Call.

Miller, R. (2020). "The day 'all hell broke loose.' A look back at the
1971 race riot at Easton Area High School." *LehighValleyLive.*
https://www.lehighvalleylive.com/news/2020/03/the-day-all-
hell-broke-loose-a-look-back-at-the-1971-race-riot-at-easton-area-
high-school.html

Morning Call. (1989, August 6). "Pennsylvania Schools Building Boom - Top 5." *The Morning Call.*

Morning Call. (1988, April 21). "Sports Scores." *The Morning Call.* [No author specified].

Petrucci, J. (1999, March 22). "Cavaliers' Carty goes to sidelines reluctantly." *Pocono Record.*

Pocono Record. (2010, Feb. 4). "Bushkill Elementary graduates 109 from D.A.R.E." *Pocono Record.*

Pocono Record. (2000, Dec. 9). "Dimon Brown loses life in Fri. accident" *Pocono Record.*

Rothman, S. (2010, April 30). "Bushkill Elem. students show flair in school science, art fair." *Pocono Record.*

Scott, A. (2000, Dec. 10). "Newest school is dedicated." *Pocono Record.*

Seder, A. M. (2000, Aug. 24). "New E-burg school 'best of the best.'" *Pocono Record.*

Photography and Graphics

Anderson, M. G. (2000). East Stroudsburg Area SHS North Academic Shield. [Print Illustration].

Costa, A. (2004). Cast of the 2004 Spring Musical. [Still Photograph].

Costa, A. (1984). Photos of the 1984 Graduation Ceremony. [35 mm slide Photographs].

Costa, J. (2024). Athletic Hall of Fame. [Still Photograph].

Costa, J. (2024). Gifts of the Class of 2004. [Still Photographs].

Costa, J. (2024). Gifts of the Class of 2003. [Still Photograph].

Costa, J. (2007). The Timberwolves Stadium. [Still Photograph].

East Stroudsburg Area School District (2000). East Stroudsburg North Logos. [Computer Graphic Designs].

East Stroudsburg Area School District (2000). East Stroudsburg SHS North: Faculty and Staff 2000-2001. [Still Photograph].

Paolino, R. (2024). Photo of an original Timberwolf football helmet. [Still Photograph].

Roberts, T. (2001). Photos of the 2001 Graduation Ceremony. [Still Photographs].

Websites

CavalierNet (1998). http://www.cavalier.net. [Web capture retrieved using the Wayback Internet Archive].

East Stroudsburg High School North (2004). http://www.esasd.net/ehn. [Web capture retrieved using the Wayback Internet Archive].

James Glimm Obituary (2000). https://www.legacy.com/us/obituaries/star-gazette/name/james-glimm-obituary?id=38853267

Lois Ann Carty Obituary (2024). https://obits.lehighvalleylive.com/us/obituaries/etpa/name/lois-carty-obituary?id=54804482

Luzerne County Sports Hall of Fame: William Houston (1997). https://www.luzernecountysportshalloffame.com/portfolio_page/william-houston/

Mr. Dobrowolski's Virtual Classroom (2001). http://www.esasd.net/ehn/math/dobrowolskid.html. [Web capture retrieved using the Wayback Internet Archive].

Pennsylvania Teacher Information Management System. Educator Complete Profile: Anthony J. Crimaldi. http://www.teachercertification.pa.gov/Screens/wfViewEducator.aspx?P=ti0i8u6Oh+l-2RKo9llO2UQ==&S=ti0i8u6Oh+l2RKo9llO2UQ==&PH=C/aM-FRlxbhpGNYoA54R67w==

Pennsylvania Teacher Information Management System. Educator Complete Profile: Michael Michaels. http://www.teachercertification.pa.gov/Screens/wfViewEducator.aspx?P=ti0i8u6Oh+l2RKo9llO2UQ==&S=ti0i8u6Oh+l2RKo9llO2UQ==&PH=8IIxz0BcARZJZMde7/bMLg==

Pennsylvania Teacher Information Management System. Educator Complete Profile: Richard Carty. http://www.teachercertification.pa.gov/Screens/wfViewEducator.aspx?P=ti0i8u6Oh+l2RKo9l-lO2UQ==&S=ti0i8u6Oh+l2RKo9llO2UQ==&PH=fhKEHOdLGky-CB8ZpDVbDRg==

Richard Carty, Sr. Obituary (2010). https://obits.lehighvalleylive.com/us/obituaries/etpa/name/richard-carty-obituary?id=22508214

Yearbooks

Bushkill Elementary School Yearbooks, 1999-2012.

Easton Area High School Yearbooks, 1971-1974.

East Stroudsburg Area Senior High School
    Yearbooks, 1981-2000.

East Stroudsburg Area Senior High School North
    Yearbooks, 2001-2005.

J.T. Lambert Intermediate School Yearbook, 1999.

Lehman Intermediate School Yearbook, 2001.

Mansfield State College Yearbooks, 1975-1978.

Resica Elementary School Yearbook, 1995.

Williamson Junior Senior High School Yearbook, 1988.

ABOUT THE AUTHOR

Julian Costa is a 2007 graduate of East Stroudsburg High School North and was among the first class to complete grades six through twelve on the East Stroudsburg North Campus. He later attended East Stroudsburg University where he earned both the baccalaureate and graduate degrees in the Media Communication and Technology program. Over the past twelve years, Costa has taught courses in communication and computer applications at several colleges and universities in the northeastern states. His writings have been published in *American National Biography* and *Et Cetera: A Review of General Semantics*. Other works by Costa include *David Campbell: Story of a Career* (2018); *A Dream's Destination* (2020); *David's Little Town* (Editor, 2023); and *The Audiovisual Teacher* (2024).